"Why Does
He Do That?"
"Why Does
She Do That?"

Dedication

To women everywhere, who courageously ask why
and are wiser than they even know. . . .
— Dr. Paula Bloom

I want to dedicate this book to my sweet Indian mother
who's spent sleepless nights strategizing how to get me married.
After all the surprise matrimonial ads, arranged setups, and
embarrassing public commentary, "Meet my son, he's single,"
she's finally starting to enjoy my singleness. As we say, when
the time is right, it will happen. Stay strong, Mom.
— Dr. Reef Karim

Published by Sellers Publishing, Inc.

Copyright © 2012 Sellers Publishing, Inc.

All rights reserved.

Sellers Publishing, Inc.
161 John Roberts Road, South Portland, Maine 04106
Visit our Web site: www.sellerspublishing.com • E-mail: rsp@rsvp.com

Cover design by Wendy Crowell
Interior design by Heather Zschock

ISBN 13: 978-1-4162-0659-0
e-ISBN: 978-1-4162-0735-1
Library of Congress Control Number: 2011935640

10 9 8 7 6 5 4 3 2 1

Printed in the United States of America.

Cover photo credits:
Dr. Paula Bloom: photo by Clint Alexander
Dr. Reef Karim: photo by Michael Bezjian

"Why Does He Do That?"
"Why Does She Do That?"

*Two Relationship Experts
Reveal the Naked Truth About
Dating in the 21st Century*

by Dr. Paula Bloom & Dr. Reef Karim

CONTENTS

Authors' Note

We realize that in *Why Does He Do That? Why Does She Do That?* we make a number of generalizations about human behavior. Of course, we understand the uniqueness of each individual's personality and the fact that there are no one-size-fits-all solutions. However, men and women are different, and it's our intent to help readers learn how to understand those differences in order to make their relationships more fulfilling. At the same time, we know that these gender differences are not the same for all men and women; certainly, there are men who are more emotionally demonstrative (considered a typically "female" quality), and there are women who are more "results oriented" (often thought of as a "guy" trait) rather than "process oriented." What is universal is that both men and women continue to be perplexed by each other. The goal of this book is to identify some of the issues that most often frustrate and separate the sexes and to help readers learn how to overcome them. By understanding each other, we get to more deeply understand ourselves. We hope that the practical advice in this book will give you the tools you need to achieve greater happiness, health, and satisfaction in your relationships.

— Dr. Paula Bloom and Dr. Reef Karim

INTRODUCTION

Men and women are different in the way they approach dating and relationship building. Since the beginning of time, the same questions have been asked: *Why does he do that? Why does she do that?* By understanding the differences between men and women, it will be much easier for you to increase your chances of success at dating and finding a relationship that makes you happy.

With this book, you're now going to find the answers. We'll unlock the secrets to why men and women do what they do. We'll cover situations that so many of us have experienced. For example ...

Guys: Do you ever wonder why she has to consult with her friends after a date? And what do they talk about?

Ladies: Do you want to know the reasons why most men spend so little time on foreplay?

Guys: Do you wonder why she says she doesn't want anything for her birthday, and then gets mad when you don't buy her a present?

Ladies: Do you want to know why he doesn't call you after getting your number?

We are two dating and relationship experts, one male and one female: Reef is male, from the West Coast, and single, and Paula is female, from the East Coast, and married with kids. Though we have obvious differences, we share one thing in common: an expertise in human behavior. And we've each helped thousands of men and women to understand themselves and each other better. Now, we'll do the same for you.

THE EXPERTS

Dr. Reef is a medical physician with a double board certification in psychiatry and addiction medicine, and specialty training in sex and relationship therapy.

Dr. Paula is a clinical psychologist focusing on communication and relationships.

WHO WE ARE

Dr. Reef

Being a psychiatrist who's single can be both good and bad. The good is that I'm in the trenches of the dating world; I can see what's happening out there. The bad is that I always get asked the same question: *"Are you analyzing me right now?"*

Dr. Paula

Do you analyze them?

Dr. Reef

Definitely.

Dr. Paula

I'm going to ask you another question: Why aren't you married?

Dr. Reef

I've always been a late bloomer. For men, it's all about timing. It's about where they are in their life. For some guys, they're ready to be more emotionally intimate and connected at 20; for others it's in their thirties, forties, or beyond.

Dr. Paula

Is "late bloomer" code for not having found the right woman?

Dr. Reef

Absolutely. But you have to be emotionally ready to meet that person. And that emotional preparation is about career, family, and a whole bunch of other things. It's meeting the right person at the right time in your life. I haven't met her yet.

Dr. Paula

After years of dating, I met the right man for me, my husband, Steve. We each had learned from previous relationships that didn't work out. From the beginning, our relationship just flowed, and we married a few months after getting engaged. I believe there's hope for everyone to find their own Mr. or Ms. Right. Reef, you and I may have different experiences and perspectives — but, of course, that's what makes this book so unique.

Dr. Reef

Two relationship experts helping people improve their dating lives for a glorious hour or a lifetime.

Dr. Paula

Let's show readers how they can begin their search. . . .

CHAPTER 1: Your Search for a Relationship

The search begins with knowing what kind of person you're looking to meet. Have you ever thought to yourself, "I always pick the wrong people"? Have you wondered why? Is it bad luck? Or do you purposely select or attract the wrong men or women without even knowing it? In this chapter, we'll look at how men and women search for a relationship. What's worked for you? What hasn't? When we aren't aware of why we make bad choices, we run the risk of repeating old habits and patterns. A little awareness goes a long way. It's the only way for us to begin to change. . . .

What Kind of Person Do You Want to Meet?

When it comes to seeking Mr. or Ms. Right, men and women want different things. According to recent studies examining the relationship patterns of couples, most men who are "in pursuit" are hoping to find beautiful women to be their partners. Women, however, who are engaged in the same pursuit often admit that they are hoping to find men who can provide them with a degree of financial security. The irony, of course, is that while physical beauty and financial success may be attractive qualities in both men and women, and can certainly add to a person's appeal, focusing solely on one of these qualities can easily lead a person astray, causing him or her to neglect other, equally important and desirable human characteristics. Qualities like intelligence, creativity, and confidence are often the very attributes that not only help strengthen an emotional connection but also help a person succeed financially and look more attractive.

The Fantasy Trap

Dr. Reef

We all tend to objectify each other. Men are more likely to look at women as sex objects, and women are more likely to look at men as status objects. It happens. Not with everyone, but it's very common. And it's not going to change anytime soon.

Our fantasy minds can get us in trouble. We all have fantasies about the type of person we'd like to meet. But, most of the time, our ideal fantasy wouldn't be right for us. The latest Hollywood starlet may be a great person, but I guarantee you she's not right for every guy (especially if she's still in rehab). Who we *think* we want may not be the person who would make us the happiest. It's called picking the wrong people. And sometimes it's called self-sabotage when we consistently pick the same type of people who aren't right for us.

Dr. Paula

What's interesting is how we develop these "ideal types," reading fairy tales as children or falling for heartthrobs who sing songs as if directly to us. "Types" provide a way to narrow the dating field a bit. Narrowing makes things feel more manageable, but it also closes us off to opportunities.

Dr. Reef

If we look at it from an evolutionary perspective, it made sense for men to seek out the fantasy "attractive" woman (which at one time was a woman with big, child-bearing hips), and for women to find a guy who'd be a good provider (which used to be a guy who could kill things). Each sought different "perks" in order to have a better life. It served humans well at one time. But we're no longer cavemen (most of us, at least). Nowadays, the life expectancy of a relationship is dependent on getting past the clichés that hijack our thinking, so we can look for something more. The way to get out of the fantasy trap is to look for other attributes that take the whole person into account:

- Confidence
- Sense of humor
- Philanthropy
- Intellect
- Creativity
- Compassion
- Talent
- Nurturing
- Ambition
- Athletic ability

These are qualities that you may not always see right away. To find them, you need to be genuinely interested in the other person and start the conversation. It's not an interview, it's a discussion. Don't interrogate with an agenda. Just learn about the other person and don't get distracted by their appearance or social status.

For example, let's see how Craig tries to find ways to connect with Liz on a first date, asking her about possible interests that they might share:

Craig: *I volunteer sometimes at an animal rescue, and we just got this dog that's unbelievable. I'm thinking about taking him home. Do you have any pets? Have you tried volunteering anywhere?*

(Pets. Volunteering. Service. These are great to bring up to see if you and your date have mutual personal interests.)

If Liz stares blankly, Craig had better move on to the next topic.

Craig: *I'm a big sports fan. Grew up in Chicago. Used to play a lot of sports. Now, I just take a run every morning before work. Are you a sports fan? Do you belong to a gym?*

(Talking about sports, exercise, and physical health is a huge way for men and women to connect.)

If Liz looks at Craig like he's crazy, then he can try another tactic: perhaps making her laugh, or asking what she likes to read or do for fun.

(Using humor and discussing books and fun interests are

other great ways of finding common ground.)

If Craig hasn't found anything they have in common yet, and Liz isn't hard of hearing, then the date has potential for excruciating awkward silence. If it's not working out, it's still possible to learn something about the other person. Everyone has a story — even if it's not one that's compatible with yours.

It's important to give everyone a chance and to treat each date as an opportunity to get to know the other person.

A Tip from Dr. Reef

The best way to meet someone new? Adopt a dog, play with your nephews/nieces, or walk around with your grandparents. Why? Because expressing vulnerability and compassion is incredibly attractive and a great way to meet new people. If you can love something or someone and be vulnerable, it shows you're probably a good person (that's assuming you actually like dogs, children, and old people).

BEGINNING YOUR SEARCH FOR THAT SPECIAL SOMEONE

The movies always depict people "meeting cute" — accidentally getting into the same cab or being brought together by a stray dog. In reality, happy coincidences do occur that turn strangers into romantic partners. You never know who you'll bump into the next time you go to a club or a party at a friend's house. Do some places work better for men, while others work better for women?

Dr. Reef

You can meet women anywhere. But the setting can dictate how a guy may categorize a woman: as someone who's a "keeper," a "fun girl," or a "friend." If you meet at a club, there's a much higher likelihood he'll put you in the "fun girl" category, and eventually that relationship will fade unless you both have a lot in common.

The best places to meet a woman who could end up in the "keeper" category are nonthreatening environments where an unexpected encounter might occur, such as a grocery store, the mall, or a concert — venues that both men and women frequent, which aren't usually thought of as pickup spots.

Dr. Paula

In some ways, meeting someone "unexpectedly" can be stressful for women. If a man is trying to start a conversation about a particular brand of olive oil, she might assume that he really wants to know about the olive oil, instead of picking up that it's a way for him to connect. She might think to herself, *Surely, he's not interested. I'm wearing a baseball hat and have no makeup on.* When women don't feel like they look attractive, they mistakenly assume that others won't find them attractive either.

Sometimes, women purposely go out looking "not so cute" in order to keep men away. This way, they can focus on what they need to do.

Dr. Reef

But, if a guy approaches a woman who's wearing a baseball cap and no makeup in a grocery store, then he likes her irrespective of whether she wears makeup or how she's dressed. A lot of guys like women who have a natural beauty. And picking out food together could lead to a potential date. *"You like Cap'n Crunch®? Where have you been all my life?"*

Dr. Paula

Everyone has to eat, right? We spend more time buying food than we do partying at bars and clubs. (Well, at least most people do.) Food shopping provides many more opportunities than bars to meet a wide range of people. The club scene just isn't for everyone. The grocery store? Pretty universal.

Dr. Reef

Bars and clubs are easy places to meet people but there usually isn't much long-term relationship potential there unless you really get to know the other person when you're sober. Nightclubs are fantasy land. It's all about people getting dressed up, women in hot outfits, people showing off, drinking, and dancing. There's good music, it's dark, and it's a pretty easy place to meet people or hook up. But most of the time, the people you meet at the club aren't the same fun people when they're sober in the light of day.

And many guys have this story: *"I met the woman of my dreams at a club, we spent hours talking about our families and work, and then we danced the rest of the night. It was amazing. I was so excited that I called her the next day and she was like, "Who are you again?"* Alcohol impairs memory and judgment.

Advice from Dr. Paula: *The Best Places to Meet Mr. Right*

I've heard a lot of creative suggestions from people about the best ways to meet men. Here are some of their best tips:

- Your local grocery store (check what kind of food is in their cart!)
- The art museum (watch out for those "don't touch" signs!)
- The workplace (but remember, office romances can be tricky in all kinds of ways)
- The airport (take the earbuds out, stop checking Facebook, and keep an eye out for possible dates passing by!)
- A fitness club or gym (a little bit of sweat can be sexy)
- Shared-interest conventions (especially if you love *Star Trek* and want to find your Captain Kirk)

Dr. Reef

Friends' parties and house parties can be good places to meet people. There's usually a commonality to the people there (work, sports, friends, etc.), and it's usually a more intimate event.

Dr. Paula

Parties can be a great place to meet. If you're kind of shy, and the friend hosting the party is a close friend, ask ahead of time if there'll be any single people whom you might be interested in. If so, ask for an introduction that includes a reason the host thought you'd connect. For example: *"Hi Dave, I want you to meet my friend Jen. You both are big-time cyclists."* Now, you have an instant conversation starter!

Dr. Reef

If you don't have someone introducing you, here are some

ideas for icebreakers that will help start a conversation. The key is to say something that elicits an emotional reaction (preferably a positive one).

- Introduce yourself in a way that will catch her off guard. Something amusing or funny or even strange. (*"I'm Jim, and I like fish."*)
- Comment on something happening in the room. It's a shared experience. (*"I think Charlie Sheen just parked my car."*)
- Observe the environment and the other people there. (*Mention the two women wearing the same outfit or the creepy guy in the corner — unless that's her brother.*)
- Show a hint of vulnerability. (*"I kind of liked* The Notebook.*"*)
- And of course, humor always works.

You don't want to be one of those guys who hang out in the corner with a force field of other guys. And you don't want to use aggression — like planting yourself right in front of her and refusing to move until she gives you her number. That's stalker central.

Making a Connection

Body language, flirting, teasing texts, winks, or an admiring glance are all part of the mating ritual of friendly nonverbal communication between men and women. This form of connection has been one of the prime ways men and women have shown interest in each other.

Dr. Paula
It's important to realize that not all forms of nonverbal

communication have to lead to a sexual connection. I think sometimes people are afraid to be flirty because they don't want the other person to immediately assume they want to have sex. You know, there's a wide range of what flirting can be, and that's a good thing. You can flirt, but it doesn't necessarily mean you want to date the person.

Dr. Reef

The flirting spectrum can extend from playful banter to full-on seduction. . . .

When a guy takes the time to remember something that you might have said or compliments you on what you're wearing, that can be flirting. For many men a big, big way to flirt is to make a woman laugh.

Dr. Paula

I love that! Who doesn't want to laugh? To me, flirting is about eye contact and proximity and looking at someone and looking away — and then looking back. Show them that you're interested . . . it's a fine art. It's not intrusive, but you make a point of letting someone know that you want to get to know them.

Dr. Reef

Absolutely. When you can be playful and witty and say something that really makes somebody laugh, that's an instant way to connect. And then, if you add just a half second of eye contact right after the laugh, it goes an incredibly long way.

Dr. Paula

Even online, flirting is used to connect with another person. People are using a lot of flirtatious postings and texts to get to know each other; they reveal a surprising amount of intimate details. But what is said in an online-dating situation may be very different from what is said when people are face to face.

Dr. Reef

There was a study on flirting from the University of Kansas, where researchers surveyed more than 5,100 men and women to learn how they communicate their attraction to another person. The study found little difference in the way men and women convey their romantic interest — with both sexes utilizing one of five different styles of flirting: polite, playful, physical, sincere, and traditional.

Dr. Paula

The polite flirt will shake your hand and focus on proper manners and take a more conservative approach (meaning, nonsexual).

Dr. Reef

The playful flirting style usually suggests little interest in a long-term relationship; it's more about boosting their own self-esteem. The physical flirt develops relationships quickly and tends to have more sexual chemistry.

The sincere flirt communicates from the heart and seeks connections that are genuine — they will look you in the eye. More women than men tend to be in this category. And finally, there's the traditional flirt. They are typically introverted and don't like crowded bars. They don't succumb to a wink or flirtatious suggestion — they go slow and tend to prefer a more intimate dating scene.

Dr. Paula

This kind of information can be very useful. With it, people can limit the risk of misunderstandings and even heartbreak by being smart and learning to read the signals they receive from another person. But there's always the chance they may not interpret those signals correctly. We are human after all, and there is no one right formula for everyone.

MISSED CONNECTIONS — A MISSED OPPORTUNITY?

A guy is walking down a crowded sidewalk, and he accidently bumps into a woman going in the opposite direction. Papers spill out of the file folder she's carrying, and they both bend down to pick them up. There's a moment when their eyes meet, and in that brief exchange they both feel a spark. They pick up the papers, she says thanks, he says good-bye, and they go their separate ways. As she hurries back to the office, she wonders, *Was that look what I thought it was?* As he watches her get lost in the crowd, he wonders, *Wow, what was that?*

That was a missed connection. There are tons of Web sites dedicated to missed connections — to people who may have briefly seen each other and even spoken with one another, and felt a spark but didn't follow through by exchanging names and contact information. They search on the Internet, hoping to find the man or woman "that got away." This seems to be a common problem for both women and men. In order to avoid the regrets of a missed connection, what can you do?

Dr. Paula

It's natural to feel a certain hesitancy when you see a stranger you're interested in. You're drawn to that other person, but you worry about putting yourself on the line and risking rejection by starting a conversation or asking for his or her phone number or e-mail address. There's a reason why the missed connections section of craigslist is so popular. Many people have to make a split-second decision — do I go for it? Or not?

Dr. Reef

Men don't have the same safety issues as women, so they are more apt to take risks. Asking a woman for her number, in this scenario, means being willing to be vulnerable and being willing to be rejected. That's not easy for some men.

Dr. Paula

What do you have to lose if you ask for her e-mail address?

Dr. Reef

Just your pride, ego, and your good mood if she says no. It depends how confident you are at that time.

Dr. Paula

So, what about the flip side? If she does the asking, will she be perceived as too forward? Also, women tend to be more risk averse than men. It's not just about emotional risk taking. If a woman has just met a guy, he may be cute and appealing, but how does she know what she's getting herself into? Can she trust her instinct? Her physical safety's at stake as well. But if she doesn't act in the moment and give him her number, will she live to regret it? Basically, it's not high risk to exchange e-mail addresses, especially those that don't reveal information about your name or where you work.

Note to self: Create an extra e-mail account just for dating — it's a great way to keep track of who's contacting you.

Dr. Reef

For men, when a woman approaches us, it really comes down to the attraction and the connection. If we're into a woman and she asks for our number, that's great. But if we're not attracted . . . then pass the awkward sauce. It can get really weird, because most guys don't want to make a woman feel bad or hurt her feelings, but we also don't want to lead her on.

Exchanging e-mails is smart on both sides. Just don't make it a cheesy e-mail address like: *princessbrittany#1@* . . . or *IgottabigoneBob@* . . .

BLIND DATES

Dr. Reef

Paula, what do you think of blind dates as a way of meeting new people?

Dr. Paula

It depends on how well the people setting you up know you. If they are really familiar with each of you, then they might have a sense of whether you'll be a good match. Sometimes things work out — but if they don't, it can create a lot of discomfort.

Dr. Reef

If it doesn't work out, there's potential for drama with the person who set you up.

Dr. Paula

A few ground rules can go a long way. For example, agree that once you've been set up, the "matchmaker" won't ask any questions about how it went. You don't want to keep going out with someone who isn't good for you out of fear of losing a friend. When things don't work out, it's easy for everyone to get emotional and take things personally.

Dr. Reef

That's true — there's nothing worse than an overly emotional matchmaker.

Why Did I Do That?

Dr. Paula

At this point, we're going to ask you to hit your personal "pause" button and think about who you've been dating in the past and why things didn't work out. Did you go after people that weren't good for you? Before we start trying to figure out why he or she does something, we need to understand ourselves and the reasons why we've made some of the choices we made.

Dr. Reef

To be more effective in your future dating life, you have to understand your past. We all develop specific dating habits and are conditioned to respond in certain ways based on our history (emotional reactions may include being sensitive, competitive, dismissive, sarcastic, etc.). Don't make the same dating mistakes again and again. Be present on the date and get a sense of when your automatic emotional reactions start kicking in and what you can do to stop them from taking over. You'll be less self-destructive and probably happier. And whether you're looking for a long-term relationship or a short-term fling, you'll be more likely to attract what you're looking for — and be on the same page with him or her.

Dr. Reef: Your *"Why Did I Do That?"* Dating Profile

By reflecting on the questions below, you'll have a better sense of your dating habits. Understand what you've been doing in the past and you can make changes in the future. If something hasn't been working before — whether it's where you've been going on a date or what you've been wearing — it's time to rethink it and try a different approach when you date someone new.

1) Where did you go on your last date?

For instance, if you went to a movie, there's less opportunity to talk and feel more comfortable with that person. But if you're shy, a movie might be a shared experience that can elicit further conversation. A bar is great as a social atmosphere, but there are many distractions, and alcohol can mask or alter feelings and chemistry. Dinner is a shared experience that provides time to talk.

2) What did you wear on your last date?

How you dress has an impact — not only on how you look but also on how your date perceives you. For women, being too sexy can be distracting, and too dressy can be read as uptight or formal. Dressing in clothing that's comfortable will help you be more yourself. Of course, how you dress often depends on the setting. For guys, it's important not to dress too casual for the date, as it could be read that you don't care.

3) Who did most of the speaking?

A date is about two people getting to know each other. It should not be a brag session for one person or an interviewing session for another. It's very important that both people feel heard and both people are able to express themselves. "Bulldozers" are good for building houses, not relationships.

4) What did you find out about your date?

Although it's not a formal interview, it is important to gather enough information about commonalities, chemistry, and interests to gauge whether you should go out again. It's also important to know what you're looking for — a couple of fun dates or the potential for a long-term relationship?

5) Was there a lot of sex talk in the conversation?

Sex is a very easy topic to discuss and can give you a false sense of intimacy and commonality. It's a universal subject. If guys talk about sex too much, they can scare the woman away. For women, too much sex talk can distract a guy and prevent him from getting to know the real you.

FAMILY MATTERS

Dr. Reef

It takes strength and courage to have enough insight to look at your past and take ownership of patterns, behaviors, and habits that need to be changed. And to do that, we need to go back — way back, to who we were before we became the adults we are now. You may not think that how you were raised has anything to do with your dating habits, but research shows that it has much more influence than you may think. How you connected as a child to your parents impacts how you relate as an adult to the people you date.

Dr. Paula

The early connections you made (or didn't make) with your parents (or whoever else may have raised you) have a lasting impact. Yes, something that happened over 20 years ago can affect what will happen 20 minutes from now.

Dr. Reef

That's the reason why psychiatrists and other mental-health practitioners always say, *"Tell me about your childhood"*; what they mean is, tell me about your emotional relationships when you were growing up. Those relationships are all about attachment — how you connected as you were growing up. We look at your development history and the pattern of attachment you had with your primary caregivers (usually your mom and dad) and siblings.

If your parents' relationship was a nightmare, it doesn't necessarily mean you're a lost cause. Practicing how to connect and be emotionally intimate with friends can help you be ready for a romantic relationship. Of course, the romance and sex won't be there, but the concepts of trust, loyalty, and honesty are the building blocks of a strong connection with another person.

Dr. Paula

As much as we don't like to admit it, our past influences our present.

Dr. Reef: Your *Family-Connection* Profile

Consider the questions below and answer them to get a better understanding of your emotional-connection history. As you reflect on your responses, you'll begin to understand why you've related to some of your romantic partners in the ways you have. For example, if you answer "no" to the first question below, you might see how not being loved or encouraged as a child may have contributed to your adult habit of seeking constant praise — perhaps texting a boyfriend or girlfriend too frequently for reassurance.

If you answer "no" to the first two questions, it doesn't necessarily mean you have a major problem. It's just good information to discuss with your friends or a therapist.

1) Were you complimented, encouraged, and loved as a child?

Not having this in your childhood could lead to an adult who is needy and constantly in search of validation from others.

2) Were your emotional needs met?

If your general emotional needs weren't met, you may have become accustomed to not being emotionally cared for, and this could affect your self-esteem as an adult.

3) Were your parents controlling, manipulative or unstable?

An unstable emotional history in childhood could lead to pathological drama and chaos as an adult. And controlling parents could lead to "acting out" against emotional intimacy as an adult, particularly in men.

4) What was your role in the family (big sister, babysitter, the smart one, the little one, etc.)?

Your role in your family may determine your comfort level and the role you take in dating as an adult.

5) How did your family handle conflict?

Conflict-resolution styles that were learned in your early years are often repeated in adulthood. If you yelled, used sarcasm, were physical, or would withdraw during conflict when you were young, this may show up again in your dating and relationships as an adult.

6) Did you experience any type of trauma growing up?

Trauma can cause many types of emotional disturbance as an adult.

Note from Dr. Reef and Dr. Paula: We want to emphasize that your answers shouldn't be used to justify or rationalize behavior that may be unhealthy; you can blame your childhood for so long until you start making active changes. But it's incredibly important to understand your emotional background. Just because you know why you do what you do doesn't mean you should continue doing it. Also, it doesn't mean you can't make efforts to change your behavior to relate to others in a more positive manner. And there's always help from professionals as well. So, if you're constantly seeking praise from your date because you felt unloved as a child, you can take steps to transform this need. Try to limit the number of times you ask for praise. Be aware of all the signs your boyfriend or girlfriend gives that you are loved. As you change your behavior, you will feel better — and your relationship will improve as well.

Add an "S" and It's "Smother"

Dr. Reef

If a man had a critical mother when he was growing up, it could have an impact on how he relates to women. Critical mothers rarely allow their kids to express themselves or think independently. It's not about the kids; it's all about mom. And her issues could stem from a history of abuse, a personality or mental-health problem, a troubled marriage, or some type of unresolved internal conflict.

As her son grows up, he may still hold the memory of being in a nondating, nonsexual relationship with a critical, controlling female where he never got his way, never had his needs met, and always felt like he was being kept in check. When he starts dating in his late teens or early 20s, he usually comes on strong and gets physically intimate pretty fast, and his girlfriend may read that as "everything is good" and he's into her. But when things begin to get emotionally intimate, the unconscious memories kick in, and he fears that his girlfriend is going to be critical or not allow him to be himself — just like his mother did. So he slowly backs away or runs in the opposite direction. His girlfriend has no idea what just happened; she may even blame herself.

It's called "fears of envelopment": the threat of being swallowed up by another person. This can be changed (with therapy or a good amount of insight), but he has to recognize the problem first. Otherwise this pattern may continue on throughout his dating life.

Dr. Paula

The fear of being swallowed up by another person is painful. Many struggle with this issue; intimacy with another person can feel almost impossible. The good news is that these fears can be helped and the behaviors relearned. On a daily basis, I see clients confront old issues and replace them with new experiences.

Dr. Reef

Some guys date women who remind them of their mother, as a way to try to fix their "unconscious conflicts" that are still ongoing (with their mother). They can't "fix" their mother, so they find someone like her and try to "fix" her. It sounds crazy, but it happens.

If you date the opposite of your critical, controlling mother, then you've reached a point in your mother-son relationship where you want a different way of relating to a woman. There's no right or wrong answer. It's just important to know why you're doing what you're doing.

A Tip for Men from Dr. Paula

If you're dating a woman whose dad was emotionally absent when she was a child, it may play out in her present relationship with you. As the two of you become closer, that relationship with her father is going to resurface at some point. It may happen as you're preparing to travel on a business trip or a weekend away with your friends; you notice her insecurity and that she needs reassurance you'll keep in touch with her while you're gone.

Dr. Paula: *Case in Point*

Recently, a client was sharing with me his struggle with anxiety. Whenever he was presented with a new project at work (he is very bright and competent), he became anxious and unsure of himself. He would get sweaty, shaky, and tongue-tied when one of his bosses would talk to him about anything new. It was the same reaction when he went on dates. Any time he was dealing with something unknown (to him, unknown = risky), his body and mind told him it was dangerous. Some people see opportunities as adventures, and others see the unexpected as land mines — he was the land-mine type.

As we talked about his childhood, he realized that his mom never let him take risks; he didn't learn to ride a bike, he never learned to swim, and he wasn't allowed to go on any overnight camping trips. He didn't get the experience of falling down and learning that he could pick himself back up. After some talking, reflecting, and journaling, he realized that he wasn't really scared of the project, but rather he feared what would happen if he failed at it. He started taking more risks, and he was seeing success. His track record of trying something new and succeeding kept getting stronger. He even failed a few times, but he saw that the world didn't fall apart when that happened. He not only survived, he thrived.

"Fall seven times, stand up eight." — Japanese proverb

Dr. Paula

A lot of women have some unanswered questions about their relationship with their dad. Men use the term "daddy issues" to refer to a woman who is very needy: "I guess her dad didn't give her enough attention, and now she needs me to call her five times a day and tell her I love her all the time." Yes, some women do seek the attention of men if they didn't get enough as a child. And yes, some women date older men for the same reason. But there are lots of people who grew up without a father and go on to have healthy relationships with men. What's important is that you be aware of how much of your reactions to the current guy might really be meant for your dad.

Dr. Reef

Some older men and younger female relationships work. But many don't, because it's more about the past "issues" than it is about the current relationship.

Dr. Paula

It can go a few different ways. On one hand, a woman who's familiar with how it feels to be neglected may be subconsciously attracted to men who trigger this response in her. It's what she understands. Kids also have a tendency to idealize their parents. If you thought your dad was perfect, you might hold out for the perfect man (who we know doesn't exist). You aren't looking for someone like your actual dad, but more someone like the fantasy your childhood self created. Unfortunately, we tend to be drawn towards what we know even if we know we don't like it.

Dr. Reef

We all have residual patterns from our childhood that leave a behavioral imprint on our actions and decisions. And it's an important thing to think about when you look at how you date. We all develop a dating style; the way we emotionally react. Most of the time we just do it without thinking about why. But if you're having dating problems, then it's important to ask "why" and do some research on your previous dates and your childhood to look at your habits, conditioning, and patterns. Make sure to reflect on the questions in "Your 'Why Did I Do That?' Dating Profile" and "Your Family-Connection Profile" in this chapter.

Dr. Paula

Knowing yourself and being willing to tell yourself the truth lead to being able to show up more fully in your relationships. Also, remember: your past has more power when you aren't aware of it. I've heard it said, "That which we resist persists." Just because you've been through painful relationships in the past doesn't mean you are doomed to misery in your future. You have the ability to transform your pain into great power. One of my favorite definitions of luck is: Luck is where preparation meets opportunity. In this next chapter, we'll help you prepare to make your own opportunities. "Lucky in love" is not just for the "lucky."

So, we've begun to look at some of the differences between men and women that you need to be aware of as you think about dating. Those differences might seem mysterious and overwhelming at first, but we'll help you get to the point where things become clear.

Read on. . . .

CHAPTER 2: Dating Prep 101

In the last chapter, we discussed where to meet people, how to make the initial approach, and the importance of asking yourself about your family history and past dating habits — to help you make better choices in the future. In this chapter, we help you gain more clarity about why men and women do what they do on the first date. We all have our own individual dating patterns and habits, but there are also specific gender-based decisions, expectations, and ways of preparing for a date. We'll look at how men and women may approach a date in very different ways.

Do Men Date Differently Than Women?

 When Chris met Tina at the Apple store, he thought she was cute and liked her sense of humor so he asked her out.

Tina's excited to be going on a first date with Chris. She's spent hours getting herself ready and obsessing over every detail — her dress, shoes, hair, and makeup. She even brought in her girlfriends to serve as her "date advisory board." The consensus was to wear a sexy tight dress and high-heeled shoes. Sure, she had to keep pulling the dress down, but they reassured her, "You look hot!"

Chris doesn't spend much time preparing for the date. He goes to the gym, drives home, showers, puts on jeans and a T-shirt, and heads out to the restaurant. Total prep time: about 20 minutes., He gets there first and orders a drink from the bar.

This is just an example of one couple, but it can provide insight into the mind of a typical man and woman.

Dr. Reef

Tina and Chris are probably both a little nervous, but it may come across in different ways. Tina was asking for the support of her girlfriends. It's the beginning of her story. Chris was keeping his expectations low. Dating can be really fun, but since you don't really know the other person and you have no idea how things are going to go, it can be anxiety provoking.

Dr. Paula

And the more nervous they are, the less they'll be able to be themselves. The pressure's on to make a good impression.

Dr. Reef

Chris gets to the restaurant first and orders a drink from the bar. Many people use alcohol to calm their nerves or to just relax, and sometimes it works, but it can also backfire. It can make you more impulsive, more emotional, and you may say something "too soon" ("You look good in leopard") or something not exactly appropriate for a first date.

Dr. Paula

What a woman wears has a great impact. On one hand, she wants to look sexy, and on the other hand, she wants to make sure he gets to know her.

Dr. Reef

As Tina keeps playing with her dress, Chris starts to stare. He likes the dress, but it's distracting, and he notices that Tina doesn't look that comfortable. Men are visual creatures; they're hardwired to respond to a woman's physical appearance. Tina's dress caught his attention. Now, it's time for him to learn more about her. Hopefully there's a lot to learn; otherwise the focus is going to revert back to the dress.

Dr. Paula

Men and women often have a hard time "reading" each other's signals, especially on a first date, when they're trying to take in so much new information coming at them all at once. As we take a look at their conversation, let's see if certain signals get misinterpreted.

Tina: *So what do you like to do for fun?*

(This is her way of finding out how much they have in common.)

Chris: *I restore old cars and hike.*

(He's answering her question.)

Tina: *Oh, where do you go hiking?*

(She feels the need to initiate questions and keep the conversation going.)

Chris: *By my house. Want another drink?*

(He's having a couple of drinks early in the date and isn't asking about her.)

Dr. Paula

It's just the beginning, but notice that Tina doesn't mention a thing about her interests — she's looking to learn more about Chris, but she's forgetting to let him know about herself as well. She's getting resentful that not once does he ask about her (unless you include his offer for another drink).

Dr. Reef

Chris is using alcohol to relax on the date. He's also trying to get Tina to drink. He's only answering questions but not learning anything about her. Men will readily answer questions when asked but don't usually ask as many questions as women do early on. Men are much more inclined to flirt, use eye contact, and talk about themselves in the beginning.

Dr. Paula

While women are comfortable asking the questions (it's an important part of how women support each other), they also want to be listened to.

Dr. Reef

The longer he doesn't know anything about her, the more he may comment on her appearance.

Dr. Paula

And the more he drinks and comments on her appearance, the more uncomfortable she becomes. She's then even less likely to reveal who she is.

Dr. Reef

This date will have a much better outcome if he starts learning more about her and chills out on the drinking. There needs to be some sort of comfort level by the end of this first date to have a second one. It's both their responsibility to make the other feel comfortable and learn about the other person.

Dr. Paula

The irony is that they won't even get to find out how much they really do have in common with each other.

Dating Tips from Dr. Paula

- Control your nerves so they don't control you.
- When you are seeking to learn more about the other person, remember to share something personal about yourself as well.
- Drink in moderation — so you can zero in on the conversation rather than zone out.

Advice from Dr. Reef: *Seven Things Guys Probably Shouldn't Say on a First Date*

---

1) Can I borrow some money?
2) You should work out.
3) I'm going to need to know where you are at all times.
4) I've been thinking of names for our kids.
5) My probation officer is meeting us later.
6) I'm excited to have sex with you tonight.
7) What was your name again?

Dr. Reef

Let's look at another example of a man and woman on their first date to see why open communication is crucial to making connections.

 Brendon and Melissa met at the gym. They hit it off, and Brendon asked her if he could take her to dinner. Melissa said yes and was excited to be going out with someone whom she felt so attracted to. After being seated at a booth, Melissa doesn't know why Brendon is taking so much time looking at the menu.

Melissa: *I love the atmosphere here. It's really cool. Have you been here before?*

(This is Melissa's way of drawing Brendon's attention away from the menu.)

Brendon: *Couple of times.*

(He's studying the menu. He knows Melissa is a vegetarian,

so he's worried there may not be a good vegetarian dish for her, and also . . . he really wants to order a steak.)

Dr. Reef

Melissa doesn't have ESP. She won't know why Brendon is so taken with the menu unless he opens up and tells her. But she could also discuss the menu with him since he's so focused on it. That may elicit a shared experience, since they both have to order.

Dr. Paula

If she knew that he was trying to make sure there were items on the menu she could eat, she'd realize he cares about her.

Dr. Reef

Let's look at an alternative way the conversation could have gone:

Melissa: *I love the atmosphere here. It's really cool. Have you been here before?*

Brendon: (looking up from the menu to make eye contact with Melissa) *Couple of times. But when I've come here before I never paid much attention to the menu. I know you're a vegetarian, and I want to make sure they have something you like on the menu.*

Melissa: (moved by how thoughtful he is) *That's very sweet of you. They have some good salad and pasta dishes. Sounds delicious.*

Brendon: *Good. So, quick question, can I order a steak?*

Dr. Reef

In this scenario, he communicated more effectively and let

her know what he was thinking. That way, they were on the same page and there was less room for misunderstanding.

Dr. Paula

Exactly. What a difference! It took the conversation in a whole new direction, with both of them feeling more connected to one another.

Dr. Reef

Sometimes, men don't want to appear vulnerable, so they may keep their emotions and communication locked down.

Dr. Paula

When women feel nervous, they tend to have one of two reactions: either stop talking or start asking a ton of questions. When she is in charge of the questions, it gives her a sense of being the one in control, because she can talk without really revealing too much about herself. Women sometimes put up a wall to protect themselves. It's a way for them to feel safe; men feel the wall has been put up to keep them out.

Dr. Reef

It's important to learn more about each other and ask questions, but if it goes too far and a woman starts asking too many questions because she's curious, nervous, or wants to make an informed decision about whether she wants to continue going out with him, it may come across like an interrogation. A guy may react by only providing minimal information or one-word answers.

She asks how his week went. He says, "Fine."

Dr. Paula

What you call "interrogation" may actually be the woman's way of communicating with the guy, of finding out more about him. But instead of sharing much about his life, he just shuts down.

Dr. Reef

Dating should not be a research project. After she's figured out that the guy's not a serial killer, it's time for her to stop *actively* gathering data. It's now time for her to trust and be in the moment and see if the two of them connect. Being on the receiving end of an interrogation is no fun at all . . . in war or in dating. If your energy is on the "interview," you're not going to be open to the real-time connection.

Dr. Paula

Are you saying that guys don't gather data, too? What about when he's looking at her legs, dress, and breasts?

Dr. Reef

Men gather data, too, but it's usually not as direct or confrontational. And men also need to keep the visual in check, because if it's too obvious, they'll come across as creepy.

Dr. Paula

What can kill the date is when he doesn't interact. If he's unresponsive, she's going to think she's said the wrong thing or that he doesn't like her.

Dr. Reef

My advice is to simply be present, to be there on the date, and to stop trying to prematurely figure things out. Some of the best conversations that people have on dates are about what's happening in the room at that moment in time. The shared experience is the key to dating. That's the best way for a connection to happen. You can bond with someone in a heartbeat when talking about the girl grinding against a speaker or the old guy in the *Miami Vice* outfit or the superloud drunk guy in the corner.

Share the experience of what is going on around the two of you when you're on a date. Be in the now rather than in the past or future.

Dating Types to Avoid

Dr. Reef

With each new relationship, people often fall right back into the same old habits and patterns that got them into trouble in the past. There are many types of guys out there, but here are four "types" that most women might want to avoid:

The "Eye Candy" Guy

The guy gets so caught up in how a woman looks that it lights up the primal circuits in his brain, and she soon finds out that she's on a date with a caveman who wants to know nothing about her except whether she has a full-body spray tan.

Dr. Paula

Women will do that, too — a gorgeous man walks into a room, and silence descends. It's almost a holy moment.

Dr. Reef

When a guy is too focused on the visual, he starts to objectify in a unidimensional way. The focus is all on sexuality and not on the internal connection. So he ends up learning very little about her.

Dr. Paula

He's not interested in her mind? How smart or accomplished she may be? If that's the case, he's someone to steer clear of — unless, of course, she has a fling on her mind and nothing more. How can she recognize a guy like this?

Dr. Reef

It's pretty simple. He won't ask many questions, and he'll comment on her physical appearance throughout. All guys will notice the external, but good guys will also ask about other qualities. The "eye candy" guy prides himself on his attractiveness and will primarily focus on the woman's attractiveness. It's all about the external. And it doesn't take a lot for him to move from one woman to another, because he doesn't connect internally with any of the women he meets.

Dr. Paula

What are the other three?

Dr. Reef

Next on the list is:

Mr. Insecure

Some men are unsure of themselves in the company of women. Generally, it's not something he wants to show, so he'll overcompensate by bragging or spending tons of money to impress his date. This guy is not super egocentric, just insecure. He isn't hopeless, but it may take perseverance to get to know him.

Mr. Egocentric Narcissist

He'll spend the entire date talking about himself. He won't show much interest in her besides the obligatory nod or brief response. It's all about him because he needs to self-soothe and hear himself speak. It's not that he's not interested in you. He just needs to make sure he's emotionally okay first. These guys need a lot of validation. Imagine somebody at home complimenting himself in front of a mirror . . . that's this guy. This is, as you can guess, a problem with insecurity or particularly with the inability to emotionally connect with another person.

Mr. Needy

Yes, guys can be needy, too — especially if they're broke, don't have an apartment, have mommy problems, or aren't over their ex-girlfriend. A red flag is if he talks too much about his ex or tries too hard to please. Or asks to borrow money. Of course, for a woman who likes to rescue people, he may be perfect. But a relationship with him usually won't last long or be fulfilling, unless you want to take care of someone or have him rely on you.

Dr. Paula

Reef, besides the four types you've just named, is Mr. Bad Boy on your list?

Dr. Reef

What is it about bad boys? I know a woman who broke up with a Harvard grad — a super good-looking, funny, and charismatic guy, but he wasn't "edgy" enough. She then started dating a guy who had a Harley, no job, and was covered in tattoos. What's the attraction to these guys?

Dr. Paula

A girl's need for excitement can cover a broad range. Some say that they get bored with nice guys. Others reason that bad boys come off as very confident. Confidence is sexy. Some even think, *He's a bad boy now, but I'll be the woman who can tame him.* The challenge of trying to change someone can be somewhat futile and draining, but the dare can be interesting to a woman.

Dr. Reef

That's usually a losing battle. Especially if you're "taming" a guy who's out of work, lives with his mom, and has a prison record.

Dr. Paula

I agree, it can be painful.

Society romanticizes bad boys — they are where the fun and adventure lie. But more often than not, bad boys don't treat women very well, and those women with low self-esteem can fall hard for that type of guy. How can she break this habit? By being honest with herself about what her past experiences with bad boys were really like — how she was hurt or used by them. As we said before, it's easy, in retrospect, to remember only the good. I advise clients to give friends and family permission to hold a "relationship intervention," to remind her of how much pain the bad boys caused — and how her misery affected her relationships with so many others. I ask her to think about what having a bad boy for a husband (or potential father to her kids) might be like.

Of course, just as women are attracted to bad boys, men are sometimes drawn to:

Ms. Bitch

Reef, this is something you may be familiar with.

Dr. Reef

Personally or professionally?

There's an air of romance surrounding bad boys, and I think the same is true about "bitches," perhaps even more so. Look, bitches and bad boys are great to "date" if you don't take things too seriously — and you don't expect to have a long-term relationship. Otherwise, you'll get your heart broken unless they change. The stereotype is that "bad" = someone that's novel, fun, rebellious, naughty, dangerous.

I don't think most "bad boys" or "bad girls" are really that dangerous — most are just expressing themselves in their own unique way. Party girls exude fun, and they don't care about anything except alcohol, getting into clubs, and dancing on a speaker. The men that love bitches enjoy their apparent lack of neediness. Bitches are a challenge. They don't seem like they're interested, and that makes men curious. Men love party girls — but not forever. Party girls have an expiration date.

Bad Dates

Bad dates make for interesting stories . . . if you only have one or two. But if you've had one disaster story after another, keep on reading . . .

Men and women can react differently to the shock and awe of bad dates. Both men and women try to distract themselves, hang out with friends, or try to find new people to date. Guys may tell you that they get over bad dates quickly — "out of sight, out of mind" — but is that really the case? Or are the memories just in hiding, only to spring to mind when a new date comes into the picture? Women will tell you that the dates they've been on in the past can make them feel discouraged or even disinclined to date again. So is it any wonder that when men and women go on a new date, they sometimes feel hopeful as well as battle scarred? If you're thinking too much about dates from your past, you may need . . . a date detox.

Advice from Dr. Paula:
How to Tell If You Need a "Date Detox" . . .

❑ Yes ❑ No   Do you still have your former date's contact info programmed in your phone?

❑ Yes ❑ No   Is he or she still on your speed dial?

❑ Yes ❑ No   Do you cyberstalk any dates from your past?

❑ Yes ❑ No   Do you ask your friends to give you updates on any status changes on a former date's Facebook page?

❑ Yes ❑ No   Are you going to old hangouts in hopes of seeing a former date there?

❑ Yes ❑ No   Do you find yourself comparing every new date to one from the past?

If you answered "yes" to one or more of the questions above, follow Dr. Reef's Rx:

Advice from Dr. Reef: *Four Steps to a Successful Date Detox*

---

1) Live in reality and not fantasy, and be accountable. Talk to your friends and family honestly about why the relationship didn't work.
2) Make that reminder list of why things didn't work out and why that person is not right for you, and put it up somewhere (mirror, refrigerator) so you can look at it every day.
3) Stop watching Lifetime movies all day. It won't help.
4) Be active — go out with your friends, and look hot. Even if you don't feel hot. Fake it till you make it.

CREATING RELATIONSHIPS IN THE 21ST CENTURY

Dr. Reef

One of the things that are definitely changing the dating world is technology. But the basic concept of connecting with another person hasn't changed — it's the way that we meet each other that has changed.

Dr. Paula

Can you imagine what it was like to date before the Internet? No Googling or stalking Facebook pages and Twitter feeds. You actually had to get information about the person sitting across from you while you were on the date. And you didn't have to worry about pretending not to know things about the other person from your online sleuthing.

These days we can find almost any information we want with the click of a mouse (or a touch of our phone's touch screen). We are used to quick information and quick connections.

Technology changes much more than people do.

Sometimes, we forget that human relationships are just that, relationships. We are not used to allowing things to unfold or develop. We expect instant chemistry and that our date will have an immediate understanding of who we are. This timetable can create unrealistic expectations, making dating and relationships a very frustrating experience.

Dr. Reef
Electronic relationships are not real relationships. But Internet dating can be a way to enhance the numbers game. Some people are really into it. And many are successful. It's all about the profile.

Dr. Paula
Yes, but people aren't always as up-front as they should be. A lot of times they don't have very accurate pictures of themselves on their profiles — they post photos of when they were a lot younger or thinner or whatever. You have to decide how much of a relationship you're looking to cultivate. If you're looking for something long term, you don't want to start off with a false first impression.

Dr. Reef
I agree that some people aren't very up-front with their pictures or profiles. A man might meet an amazing woman online, or he could end up with a first date whose picture is from 1984, plus she has a crazy ex-boyfriend and wants a lock of his hair.

If you're looking for something long term, it's probably important to get the basic stuff out in the open, like if you have kids or you're in recovery. But if you're just looking to casually date, I don't think it's necessary to reveal too much (unless it's going to be obvious on the date . . . like if he wants to go drinking all day, and you're in recovery. Of course, you might want to proceed with caution if his idea of a good first date is drinking all day, whether you're in recovery or not).

Dr. Paula

I tell my clients that if they have a specific issue that they know somebody can take issue with — whether it's a woman with kids or a man who's really short — they have to decide whether they are going to reveal this before they go on a first date. Ultimately, each person has to figure out how important it is for him or her to put that information out there.

With online dating, there's a kind of old-school courting that goes on: long before two people meet in person, there's often a lot of written communication back and forth, and — with the exception of the photos on someone's profile — they're not necessarily being impacted by somebody's physicality.

My clients have described the connection that can form through texting, which can be pretty intimate. Men and women are texting personal details to people they've never actually met. A client recently told me, "We're texting six or seven times a day, and I think we are going to go out on a first date." And I thought, *Wow, there's something positive in that — that you get to connect in this way.* Of course, when you do meet, there's this anxiety that you've created these expectations and projected all this stuff onto the other person. Then you actually meet, and there can be a shock when you see the person face to face for the first time!

> **A Tip from Dr. Paula**
>
> Be sure to carefully review any text messages before you hit "send." Auto-correct has a mind of its own, and sometimes, it's a dirty little mind.

Dr. Reef

There's an element of fantasy when you look at somebody's photos on an Internet dating site and you read their profile. You see they like the same music as you. They like to cook. They like to dance. You share commonalities. You look at their picture and you're attracted to them, and a fantasy runs in your head and you think, this could be the one I've been looking for (whatever it is you're looking for). You start idealizing that person and planning the next five dates.

There's a certain element of fantasy in dating, anyway. But when it's there in writing and you see the photographs, and you don't really know the person at all, the level of fantasy increases.

Of course, it's hard for that person to ever live up to the expectations of your fantasies — and vice versa. I think men are going to focus a lot more on the pictures than they'll admit to. For example, if there's a shot of just the woman's face, the first thing we're thinking about is, *Why isn't there a body shot?*

Dr. Paula

I'm seeing an entire new industry that can be emerging for professional photographers — just focusing on taking pictures of women for their profiles, to make sure they get the perfect photograph.

Anyone who's creating a profile for an Internet dating site should have some friends look at it and give their feedback. Because you're so close to the profile, you can have a hard time being objective. Sometimes, you may not even realize that you're putting a very negative impression out there. Ask a few people you can trust to check it out and give you their honest, constructive opinions.

Dr. Reef

In addition to Internet dating, another popular way to meet people is speed dating, where you interact with a bunch of potential dates for seven minutes per person in a social setting.

Dr. Paula

It's like a test. I don't know about you, but timed tests used to make me anxious in school. It's sort of like going into a job interview. It's good to have some sense of what your talking points might be so you don't feel completely overwhelmed when you're suddenly "on."

Dr. Reef

I think speed dating is interesting. I have a friend who runs a big speed-dating service out here in L.A. It can be anxiety provoking for some people, but I also think it can be really fun for others; you get to meet and talk to a bunch of people. In many ways, it's like an interview or an audition. And if one person doesn't work out, when your time is up, you move on to the next one. And a bad "date" only goes seven excruciating minutes.

Dr. Paula

You want to be fully aware of what's going on in those seven minutes you spend with each person. Having some clarity about who you are and what kind of person you're looking for is important, too. A lot of speed dating is just not about gathering information. You're getting facts about a person, but you should also be asking yourself, *What am I feeling? Is there chemistry between us or not?*

Dr. Reef

Physical attraction is definitely a factor, but at least you have a little time to engage with someone. Speed dating works on the premise of chemistry at first sight, with seven minutes of discussion in a rapid-fire, timed setting. I like that instantaneous, impulsive rush associated with seeing a person you're interested in or feeling their energy.

Dr. Paula

There are definitely qualities that can help someone stand out in this kind of process. It's very important for a woman to be confident — as long as she's not arrogant about it. It's not enough for women to just be demure and quiet. If that's the case, the only data point the man is going to get is how you look. So, being able to put something out there about who you are is really key.

Dr. Reef

As we've said before, humor can make a big difference. If you're a guy who's funny, it can go a long way in helping you have a successful experience in the speed-dating world.

Dr. Paula

I think the reason humor works so well is because it puts people at ease very quickly. It's the beeline into a more relaxed kind of communication.

Dr. Reef

Connection is all about trust, attraction, and enjoying a shared experience. It's about feeling positive emotions; it's about laughing, feeling drawn to someone, and learning about him or her. Anything we can do to promote trust and novelty is a good thing. And knowing about our previous bad dating habits can help us to not give them power in the future.

Dr. Paula

Dating is both exciting and nerve wracking. Anxiety keeps us from fully showing up on a date. If you do some emotional preparation, and understand what hasn't worked in the past, it will help you be happier, and more successful in your dating present and future.

CHAPTER 3: The Second Date and Beyond . . .

The first date is just the beginning. If you and your date have "clicked," and you find you have a number of interests in common, the next step is to see where things go from there. At this point, you probably have more questions than answers — how do you know if the chemistry you shared on the first date will lead to something more? Is this "the one" or just a short-term fling? Will he or she call back? Men and women react in very different ways to making crucial connections, and in this chapter, we'll look at the choices that come up, and how to know whether this relationship is right or one to write off.

We'll begin by looking at the attraction or "chemistry" that occurs between two people when they first begin dating. Of course, there are all kinds of chemistry — ranging from the obvious (love at first sight) to the more unexpected (he may look like a geek, but after a while you realize how good he makes you feel when he smiles at you or makes you laugh — and your first impression changes). There's also strictly sexual attraction and the "opposites-attract" chemistry.

After the First Date . . .

The first date went well — you felt a connection and thought maybe your date did, too. How do you know if the chemistry you felt will lead to something more?

Dr. Reef

The tricky part of assessing chemistry on a first date is determining whether it's simply a short-term attraction or has long-term potential. There can be mutual attraction on a date and maybe you acted on it and "hooked up," but that doesn't necessarily mean it's going to lead to a second date or that you'll see that person again. There are many variables from the date and both of your lives that may alter whether you two go out again — alcohol, stress, previous relationships, connection, etc.

When it's right, it seems so natural for a first date to lead to a second date. But the lack of familiarity and our own individual history and baggage can change things quickly. It's hard to know if you have "chemistry" without talking about it — and you don't generally do that on a first date.

Advice from Dr. Reef: *Ten Reasons a First Date Won't Lead to a Second Date*

---

1) He's dating many other people, and you're not high priority.
2) She got drunk on the date and forgot everything you talked about, and now it's weird.
3) He or she is not emotionally available and just liked the attention.
4) He or she talked about their ex too much.
5) She constantly talked about herself in the third person. *"Stephanie is hungry. . . ."*
6) He didn't seem interested in you and was constantly checking out other girls and his phone.
7) He seemed too interested in you and mentioned how cute your kids would look.
8) He talked about sex nonstop.
9) She slipped her number to the waiter when she thought you weren't looking.
10) He can't take his eyes off of . . . ESPN.

Dr. Paula

How do you know if there's chemistry? You don't. Dealing with that uncertainty is what is so difficult.

Dr. Reef

I disagree. When you feel chemistry, you know it right away — it feels great, and sometimes it might even freak you out. It's a mixture of brain chemistry, physical response, and sharing common attributes. Everything flows, and when you start flirting with the other person, you're suddenly intrigued, energized — you have a physiological response to them, a heightened sense of awareness. Then the challenge becomes trying to figure out: *does the other person feel it, too?* It would be a little awkward to say: *"All right, we've been here an hour, let's talk about our chemistry. . . ."* So much of dating is the mystery and the fantasy, so that kind of direct communication is rare.

Dr. Paula

It could be awkward, but it's something a woman might appreciate. Women tend to become very future oriented in their thinking after a date. After one good date, a woman will start imagining what it would be like to introduce her "new boyfriend" (oh yeah, she's thinking of him as her boyfriend already) to her friends and family, even though you don't know how the other person feels. So perhaps talking about it could deflect this tendency. Reef, what do you think?

Dr. Reef

I think a conversation about chemistry could help them to know if they're really compatible, but it also takes the novelty and mystery out of the process. Dating would be easier if people were more straightforward, but that doesn't happen. Instead, after a date they usually talk to their friends and mention there was really good chemistry and they hope to go out with that person again. But as you said, the other person may not share those feelings, even if it seemed like he or she had a good time.

Sometimes, it's not really chemistry — it's the situation and environment that make them feel the "buzz" of the date. The date could seem better than it actually was because you were watching a funny comedian or listening to a great band. The event was a great fit even though the other person really wasn't. The lack of chemistry will eventually come out — if not right away, then later. I still think it's important to do something fun on a first date, so there's not as much pressure to immediately connect. But you don't want the experience of the date to overwhelm your ability to get to know the other person.

And, of course, overanalyzing a date with your friends afterwards can lead to problems as well. If they are objective and impartial, their advice can be useful, but often there's bias or they only see one side of the story *("he just wants you for sex")*, and that may influence your decision to go out on a second or third date. Your "council" of friends may be "right on" about a guy, but often their own experiences will come up in their conversation with you and assumptions will be made based on limited knowledge. The "council" influence may save you from creepy guys, or it may interfere with a potentially good connection.

Dr. Reef: *The First Date Assessment for Guys*

For every first date you go on, your "First Date Assessment" will help you to see if it was successful. Think of it as a way to get some perspective on your feelings. Reflect on these questions to determine if it's the right time to take things to the next step.

1) What did you learn about the other person that you found interesting?

2) By the end of the date, did you find yourself wanting to be closer to her (whether or not you actually acted on that feeling)?

3) Were you able to talk about yourself, and did she seem interested?

4) Did she seem emotionally available to date?

5) Was there a physical attraction?

6) Did you have some things in common? What were they?

7) Were there any absolute deal breakers for you that came up on the date?

8) Did the "experience" of the date (good or bad) greatly influence your ability to get to know her better? Was it more about the experience than the other person?

9) Did she laugh at your jokes? Was she funny?

10) Was she critical of you? Did she try to change you? Did you mention anything she should change?

Dr. Paula: *The First Date Assessment for Women*

After a date, it's important to assess how you feel. If there are things about your date that don't feel right, you have to trust those instincts. As you take time to think about the questions below, remember that this is about getting information that will help you — it's not about "judging" him. Listen to your intuition!

1) Did the date feel more like "it would never end," or did it seem to go by so fast that you wondered, *Where did the time go?*

2) Did you feel like you could relax and be yourself or did you feel on edge and uncomfortable?

3) If it wasn't perfect (which is likely the case), was there enough there for you to give it another chance?

4) Did you feel good about yourself or not so good?

5) Did you feel, *I'd really like to see this guy again?*

6) Do you find yourself wishing you had found out more information?

7) Are you curious about him and want to know more?

8) What were the major things you had in common? What were the little things you shared as well?

9) Do you feel like he was interested in what you had to say?

10) Did your intuition pick up on something weird but you can't quite put your finger on it?

Dr. Paula

You're right, Reef. There's a fine balance between trusting your own instincts and listening to the opinions of the people you trust. But your friends can't determine if you have chemistry with someone — only you can decide that. And only you can know what you're looking for at this stage of your life. He may not be "Mr. Right," but he may be "Mr. Right Now"!

THE BIG FOLLOW-UP

Nikki and Chris went on a first date and had a fun time. Afterwards, Nikki expected a call back from Chris, but she hasn't heard a word from him for a while. She runs through an internal list of possible excuses — he lost my number, he's probably very busy, maybe he's sick — but how does she know what the real reason is?

Dr. Paula

Here's the thing. Men are unlikely to give you the real reason, assuming they even know what it is. They don't want to hurt your feelings, so they want to avoid telling you. Also, if you haven't been going out all that long, they don't feel they owe you an answer.

Dr. Reef

It's commonly thought that if a woman doesn't immediately hear back from a man, it means he's just not that into her. This basically makes the woman reactive and gives the man all the power. It makes the assumption that men are linear and know exactly how they feel about a date, *and that's not true.*

Just because we're men and we have our XY chromosome set doesn't mean that we know exactly how we feel about a woman or even how we feel about ourselves after a date.

Dr. Paula

Most women are looking for a follow-up call, e-mail, or text message from him saying, "Had a great time. When can we do this again?" However, I agree with Reef — if that doesn't happen, don't immediately assume that he's not interested. You can try asking him why he hasn't called, but you need to be genuinely interested in the reason and not just trying to make an emotional plea to get him to like you.

Dr. Reef

There are so many reasons why a guy might not call or text you after a date. It might be that he doesn't know if he wants to be in a relationship. Or he's dating lots of women in rotation, or he already has a long-term relationship, or decided not to date at all. Maybe he's still working out his attachment history with their parents. He could still be figuring out if he wants to focus on his career or his personal life. And all a woman can do is to just understand that it's not something she can control, and it's best not to overanalyze.

I feel like the philosophy that the man doesn't call back because "he's just not that into you" makes everything black and white, which of course causes a woman to say, *"I just have to accept this as a loss, there's nothing I can do,"* when it might not be a loss at all. It might just be that he's waiting for her to give him a little validation, because he's feeling insecure himself about whether she had a good time. Men get fearful about rejection, and most of them fear intimacy.

Dr. Paula

But she doesn't know that. She may be feeling the same kind of insecurity about him.

Dr. Reef

After the date, a text from her that's innocuous and doesn't invade his space would be fine; something that just says, *Had a great time.* For some guys, a little encouragement from the woman he's interested in can go a long way towards making him feel comfortable enough to ask her out again.

Dr. Paula

You can even say something at the end of a date. It's a good idea to share with him if you enjoyed it. If you want to go out again, make it clear that you'd be receptive to that.

Dr. Reef

If she doesn't tell him on the date, then she should let him know soon after, like when she's driving home from seeing him, or the next day. *Definitely within the first 48 hours if it's by text.* You want to capture that special feeling when the moment is fresh.

Dr. Paula

Note to self: In general, when you contact him is not going to be what breaks the deal. What can drive him away is if you try contacting him too frequently and with too much intensity.

Advice from Dr. Reef: *Reasons Why Men Don't Call Back*

You may never know what the real reason is . . . he may not call you for any number of reasons, including:

- He's secretly married.
- He has a girlfriend.
- You're too tall for him.
- He's a serial first dater who never has a second date.
- He read your Facebook profile and didn't like your favorite music or the comment from that guy who's not wearing a shirt.
- You didn't have sex with him on the first date.
- You did have sex with him on the first date.
- You like your dog better than people.
- Your breath is bad.
- You have a cat.

The point is you may never know. Rule #1: Never try to control or change who you are to accommodate someone else so that he'll call you back. When we really like someone, we may desire to make subtle changes in ourselves over time, but not on the first couple of dates.

Rule #2: Don't drive yourself crazy trying to figure out why someone didn't call back. When it's the right time and the right person, he will call back.

Taking Things to the Next Step

Dr. Reef

A key to dating is to understand why you are dating. Are you looking to have fun? To find a relationship? To have sex? Then you should figure out what the other person is looking for, to assess dating compatibility in regard to expectations.

The first, second, and third dates are opportunities to rule out the red flags, assess commonality, have fun, and ask some direct questions. They are also opportunities to share common experiences. Remember, don't overanalyze. Know what you're looking for personally, and slowly figure out if that person works for you. For example, let's look at a scenario below.

Jim and Lisa are on their third date, relaxing on the couch in her apartment. He leans in and they kiss. After he starts stroking her hair, Lisa gets up abruptly and goes to the kitchen to make something to drink.

"Is everything okay?" Jim asks, thinking he may have misinterpreted Lisa's feelings for him.

"Everything's fine," Lisa says.

Thoughts race through Jim's mind. He's not sure how far Lisa wants to take things physically or emotionally, but he's worried about asking her. Lisa likes Jim and thinks she might like to build a relationship with him over time. Before things go further, she wants to know where she stands with him.

Dr. Paula

In this situation, Lisa has to decide what she wants and to figure out a way to let Jim know. Men and women are often wired to go at different speeds when they're dating. Jim may be in a rush to get physical. Lisa may want to dial down the pace to get to know more about him. As they continue dating, they may not always know how fast or slow to take things. Much of the stress for women in the early part of relationships has to do with not knowing "where things stand." I often hear women say things like, *"Before we have sex, I want to see if he is seeing other people. I'm scared, though, that the question will be a turnoff to him."*

There are three ways Lisa can begin a dialogue to find out where she and Jim stand in their relationship. Like with any communication, if she speaks about her feelings (using "I" to begin her sentences), she's more likely to create a space for honesty and respect with Jim.

- *"I don't want us to play guessing games with each other, so is it okay if I tell you where I'm at?"*
- *"I really want to spend more time with you, and I want to know how you'd feel about that."*
- *"I feel like things are moving really fast. Would you mind if we slowed down a little? In the past I've made the mistake of jumping in too quickly, and even though I really like you, I want to take some more time to get to know you better first."*

Dr. Reef

If Jim tells Lisa he wants to keep dating her but he wants to see other people as well, it means one of the following:

- *"I like you enough to see you again, but not enough to commit."*
- *"I need more time to get to know you. It's only the third date."*
- *"I love attention from multiple women."*
- *"I'm a total player, and you're now on my rotation."*
- *"I'm interested in you casually for fun, but I'm not interested in a relationship at this time."*

Dr. Paula

If Jim wants to see other people but Lisa doesn't, this could create conflict. It's great that he's being honest with her and telling her this. However, if they're not on the same page — if, in fact, Lisa knows that she's not much of a juggler — she needs to be honest with herself and with Jim. If she feels that it's going to drive her nuts to know that Jim is dating other women, this relationship may not be the right one for her right now. He may be dating others, but that doesn't mean she needs to date others as well.

Dr. Reef

If he's a serial dater, he'll either be honest with Lisa, or he'll mislead her into thinking he wants a long-term relationship, but it'll be pretty apparent after a while that he's dating multiple people and she's only getting one night a week or less. If a guy is in it for fun and to have sex, he might not tell a woman his true intentions because he fears she won't go out with him. Serial daters could have bad intentions, or they might be good people (if they're honest) who just aren't ready to settle down, are only looking to have fun, or are scared to get in a relationship.

Dr. Paula

If Jim tells Lisa he wants to date others as well as her, she needs to let him know if she's okay with that. If she is, it's completely reasonable for her to tell him that she'd appreciate knowing if he's sleeping with others. *"No sex before monogamy,"* as The Millionaire Matchmaker likes to say!

Planning the Date

 Peter asked Caitlin out on a first date at a Manhattan bar. He was flustered and asked too many questions, but he really wanted Caitlin to like him. For their next date, Caitlin called Peter to ask him out. "I have a surprise planned for you," she told him. She had heard him mention that he liked to go to concerts, so she bought two tickets to one that was coming up at the Beacon. When she presented him with the tickets on their next date, Peter was thrilled. Without Caitlin even knowing it, the band playing that night was one of Peter's favorites. Though he was initially reticent to let Caitlin plan the date, he was glad she did.

Dr. Reef

Most often, the guy asks the woman out. But if you poll single guys, they would be open and interested in going out with a woman who asked them out *if* they found her attractive and interesting. Peter and Caitlin had a good first date. It's fine for Caitlin to ask him out once in a while, but it's usually better for the couple if it reverts back to Peter making more of the plans. If she keeps asking him out, he may eventually get bored, because guys need to feel like they're taking the lead in the chase.

Dr. Paula

Caitlin planned something that they enjoyed doing together.
She remembered that on their first date Peter had mentioned
that he liked to go to concerts. The fact that she bought
tickets for a concert shows Peter that she was listening to him,
and could take the initiative and provide a plan of action.

Sometimes, the man might assume it's his role to plan the
dates and that's what you expect. If you want to choose what
to do on the date, tell him. If you think he might be sensitive
about this, you might want to try the following approach:
*"You have planned so many of our dates that I'd love the chance
to be able to do something for you."* Who can refuse that?

Check, Please . . .

 *Andrew knew that Mia made more money than he did,
but he still felt obligated to pay when they went out to
dinner for their first date. On their second date, Mia
was going to offer to pay, but she wondered if that would offend
Andrew. She wasn't sure if she had done the right thing by not
picking up the check.*

Dr. Paula

Men expect to pay early on but tend to like the woman
to offer anyway. As a couple gets to know each other
more, they can open up the topic for discussion. So, for
example, in the case of Andrew and Mia, when there is a
big difference in how much each person earns or is able to
spend, it should be discussed. Many women, even when
they make tons of money, like the man to treat. It's sort of

like opening doors. A woman is perfectly capable of opening her own door, but she may really prefer/enjoy it when he does that for her. Mia needs to evaluate how she really feels (and not just act the way she *thinks* she should feel) about it. Communication is where it's at.

Dr. Reef

Paying for the date can be a touchy subject if the guy makes less than the woman does, or if the guy is going on a lot of dates and is expected to pay for all of them, or if he's unemployed or having a tough time with his finances. Dating is fun unless you go broke. Any man can be chivalrous and open a woman's door. But not every man can afford to pay for every date.

Whoever asks the person out the first time should be willing to pay for the date, unless the other person offers to pay or to split the bill. Generally, the guy pays on the first date unless the woman asked him out and sets up the date. For future dates, if the woman has money, it's a great gesture to pay for something . . . dessert, the tip, drinks, half the bill. The guy is probably going to pay for the majority of the dates. Mia could offer to do that once in a while. It's a gesture that will go a long way.

THE ART OF COMPROMISE

 Danny and Jessica have been on a couple of dates and are still getting to know each other. On each date, Danny's planned the activity and Jessica's gone along with his choices, even when two of them (going hiking and traveling to an antique-car show) were not exactly things she was into. When Danny proposes going to a football game, Jessica isn't sure how to let him know that she'd rather do something else, without hurting his feelings.

Danny: (excitedly) *I have tickets to the play-off game next weekend.*

(He's not quite sure if Jessica is a football fan or not, but he knows he sure is.)

Jessica: (a little distracted) *Great . . . I've never been to a football game.*

(She has visions of sitting on cold, wooden bleachers and not knowing what's happening on the field.)

Danny: *Do you want to go?*

(He's picking up some resistance from Jessica.)

Jessica: (mustering a smile) *Sure, I do.*

Danny: *Okay, sounds good.*

(He senses that something's off, but he doesn't want to put Jessica on the defensive. He's not sure if it's the football game or if it's something about him. He's now taking it personally, and she's not looking forward to the date.)

Dr. Reef

If it's early in a relationship, you should make sure to plan a date the other person will enjoy. You don't have the luxury of sacrifice that long-term couples have. If you plan a date to do something she likes, she'll appreciate the effort you took to arrange it. A little investigation goes a long way. She may want to experience new things.

Dr. Paula

Let's see how the situation would have been different if Jessica was to let Danny know how she really felt so they could reach a compromise:

Danny: (excitedly) *I have tickets to the play-off game next weekend.*

(He's not quite sure if Jessica is a football fan or not, but he knows he sure is.)

Jessica: *I'd love to do something with you next weekend, but I have to admit that I'm not a big football fan.*

(She figures it's better to be up-front with Danny about how she feels.)

Danny: *Okay, well, I guess I could go with one of my buddies to the game.*

Jessica: *Thanks for understanding. Could we get together after the game is over? Maybe go out to dinner?*

Danny: *That sounds great.*

Dr. Paula

Because Jessica was able to express her feelings in a way that was honest but still indicated she wanted to be with Danny, they reached a win-win compromise. Planning a date takes two, and if you find yourself agreeing too often to things you don't want to do, you're setting up a pattern for your relationship that you'll regret later.

Dr. Paula: *Where Are the Red Flags?*

A 27-year-old was back on the dating scene after ending a three-year relationship. She decided that she would try the online dating thing and posted a profile. Within days she got several men interested in communicating with her. She went on one date with a guy who she felt was "a real jerk." The second man she met seemed very promising online. When they finally met in person he was all she expected, based on his profile, and all she hoped for. Oddly enough, after going on several really fun dates with him, she became very concerned. Was he a felon? No. Was he a jerk? Not at all. Was he good looking? Yup. Was he respectful? Absolutely. Was he intellectually stimulating? Totally. So, what was she worried about? *"Paula, is it a red flag that there don't seem to be any red flags?"* That simple. Her fear was that this was too good to be true. *"There must be a catch."* Not necessarily. If things seem very easy and flow early on, take that as a good sign. Who says dating has to be painful and hard?

A Tip from Dr. Reef

One of the best ways to see the "true identity" of your date is by watching the way she interacts with other people. The waiter, the bartender, and the guys standing next to you in line are all people that aren't on your date but can provide information *about* your date. Was she flirty, guarded, dismissive, sarcastic, funny, compassionate, or rude? If she's consistent, you know that's what she's probably like all of the time. If she's super sweet with you but completely different with everyone else, then she may be "acting" for you with ulterior motives.

How to Deal with a Surprising Reveal

If you're on a date and you're really into each other, what do you do when the other person reveals something about himself or herself that takes you by surprise? Do you keep dating, even though you swore you'd never become involved with someone who (has a gambling habit, has a child, is in recovery, or "fill in the blank")?

Dr. Paula

You take the information in and decide how important it is to you. Did he tell you that he has a child he's never met? How important is this to you? Is he still "technically" married but says he is going to ask for the divorce soon? Does that work for you? One person's deal breaker is not such a big deal to someone else.

You need to be honest with yourself. Does it really not matter to you that he is unemployed, or do you wish it didn't matter to you, but the truth is that it really does? Be honest.

Dr. Reef

If you want to back away from somebody gracefully, your technique should depend on how much you care about hurting the other person. If you don't care, you could just stop calling/answering their calls or just tell them you're not interested. If you do care, it may help to provide some type of explanation (the truth is always better), and it's best to do it, at the very least, on the phone.

It also depends on what the details are. If those "trivial" details are that he just got out of jail or has five kids or he's still married, then you've got a potential problem. If the details are: he cries at movies, has a mole on his right shoulder, or plays video games naked on Sundays, then maybe it's not so much of a problem.

MEETING THE FRIENDS

Dr. Paula

Meeting your date's friends is a benchmark in the relationship — but it can also be challenging and cause a lot of anxiety. A guy might introduce his date to his friends for all sorts of reasons: to get their approval, or to show her that she's important enough to be introduced to the people who really matter to him and whose opinions he respects. Sometimes, if a woman feels insecure, she may think his friends are judging her when, in fact, they may just want to get to know her.

Dr. Reef

From a guy's perspective, there are three reasons that you introduce a woman you're dating to your friends and bring her into your world:

1) She more or less forces you to do it by saying something like, *"How come I haven't met your friends?"*
2) You're not sure about her, and you think, *Well, I like her, but maybe there's a couple of things I'm not so sure about, so I'm going to introduce her to my friends and see what they think of her.* I call that the friends' "second-opinion evaluation."
3) You just want to share her with everyone in your world.

Now, the problem is that each one of these scenarios comes with different guidelines: If she forces you to introduce her to your friends and your friends love her, then all of a sudden you think, *Well, that's interesting — my friends really like her. Maybe there's something great about her that I'm not appreciating.* Or if it's a "second-opinion evaluation" and they validate that she's really great, then it may totally green-light the relationship for you. But in this scenario, if they don't like her, it could be a death sentence for the relationship if you're not totally into her.

In this third scenario, if they're not crazy about her but you really like her, you'll probably want to continue the relationship. But your guy friends may not want to hang out with her.

Dr. Paula

How the friends respond can have a big influence on your relationship and his relationship with his friends. If he thinks you're awesome and they don't particularly like you, he may feel the need to distance himself from his friends. That may have an underlying effect on how he starts feeling about life, because it's important to have time with friends and to hang out with them. It's a really key thing. But if how they feel is not in line with what you're thinking, then that could be a problem. Then again, sometimes we don't want to listen to negative input from people, even if we really trust them. Sometimes they may have ulterior motives for putting her down.

Dr. Reef

Our friends' opinions probably carry more weight than they should. If they really *know* your date, then their thoughts could matter. But if they don't really know her, then their opinions could get in the way of a good thing. Good friends should support you as you go through the dating process, not interfere.

Dr. Paula

You have *no* control about how his friends respond to you. The more you focus on it, the more miserable you'll become. The more miserable you are, the more miserable those around you will become as well. Some groups of friends are very tightly knit and take some time to allow someone new to be part of the group. Others are more open and welcoming.

Reverse your negative thinking and consider it a good sign that he is introducing you to his friends.

Dr. Reef

If the friends are standoffish, it may simply be because they don't know you yet.

If *he's into you,* he'll hype you up to them. If he doesn't want to mix his guy friendships and his relationship with you, then you need to respect that.

Dr. Paula

I agree. The most important opinion is your own. The people in your life are full of opinions that are influenced by how *they* see the world and what experiences *they* have had.

Dr. Reef

Also, his relationship with his guy friends may begin to change after he's met you. A lot of men hang out with their single male friends to watch sports, do business, or meet women. When you're in a relationship, there may be a shift in the type of friends that he hangs out with. If you're a guy who primarily goes out with your single guy friends to clubs and then you bring along your girlfriend, sometimes it can be fun, but a lot of times it can get awkward. You're thinking, *I like being out with my girlfriend, but this is a club and everyone's single and my guy friends want me to hang out with them . . .* It's entirely natural for a guy to make a shift from casual, "going out" single friends to friends in relationships. It's easier and causes less conflict. Although, every guy has that one special, single guy friend that makes his girlfriend nervous.

"Is This My S#%t or Yours?"

Justin and Carrie are at a party when Justin suddenly notices that his ex, Rachel, is there. Carrie knows that they've stayed on good terms, but nevertheless she becomes uncomfortable when she sees the way Justin lights up when he speaks with her. She gets frustrated and shuts down.

"What's the matter?" Justin asks. Carrie doesn't want him to know that she's feeling jealous and anxious. She thinks to herself, Am I making too big a deal over this chance meeting?

Dr. Paula

What Carrie's really asking herself is, *Is this about her or is it about Justin? Is this my s#%t or his?*

Dr. Reef

For Carrie to see Justin light up when he sees his ex (or anyone, for that matter) is hard, especially if Carrie's had a long history with him. In this circumstance, it would be a good idea for Carrie to run these questions by someone she's close with and who knows her well.

Dr. Paula

I'm glad to hear you say that, because there are times when sharing something like this with a friend can be invaluable. Jealousy and anxiety are normal emotions, but sometimes you can lose your perspective.

Dr. Reef

We all have dating habits and emotional triggers that can cloud our judgment or cause us to react in habitual ways. Checking in with a friend to see if it's you or the other person can provide genuine feedback. Just make sure your friend can look at both sides of the story. You don't want a "yes" man or woman here.

Dr. Paula

Don't assume that if someone still has positive feelings for a former girlfriend, that means he can't be into you and want to be with you. Be careful with thinking like that; don't confuse respect for others with an interest in wanting to get back together. Lighting up is one thing. Flirting and being all over the ex is quite another.

Taking responsibility for one's own feelings is important. A sample way for Carrie to begin a dialogue with Justin would go something like this:

Carrie: *I want to tell you that when I saw you talking with your ex, I felt kind of jealous and anxious. I really like you and, for some reason, seeing you so engaged in that conversation with Rachel made me feel uneasy.*

In this case, she's using an important formula for

communication: *When you do X, I feel Y.* She isn't blaming him. She's simply describing what she saw and explaining how she felt. He may not know that's how she was feeling. This way, instead of building up resentment and picking a fight over something else, she puts it out there immediately.

Dr. Reef

The more Justin can reassure Carrie that he's into her and not Rachel, and that he and Rachel are just friends, the easier that situation will become. This is true for any man or woman in this situation.

Dr. Paula

There are times that we may get upset about the behavior of others, even though we're doing the same thing ourselves. We may think nothing of having a friendly flirt with an ex, but we freak out when we see our boyfriend doing the same thing. The thing is, we're much more forgiving of ourselves than we are of others.

Dr. Reef

People often react in extreme ways to others who remind us of our bad traits. For example, if you weren't given much attention from your parents growing up and you developed this need for excessive validation from others, you may see that trait in someone else and immediately react negatively to that person. It's easier to do that than to look inward and make some changes in yourself.

Dr. Paula

Okay. I'm going to throw out a psychobabbleish term and then explain it: Fundamental Attribution Bias. Basically, what it states is that there's a difference in how we explain others' behavior versus how we explain our own. With others, we might assume that their "bad" behavior is a result of their personality, while with ourselves, we might explain that it has to do with external situational factors. Take driving, for example: how many times do you honk at someone and call him or her a name because they cut you off? Now, think about how irritated you get when someone has the gall to honk at you when you are trying to move over three lanes and happen to cut *them* off! That person's a jerk, but you're just trying to get off at the next exit? Hmmm.

It's true that we sometimes dislike in others what we dislike in ourselves. This is why knowing yourself is the key to forming healthy relationships.

 Katie and Connor have been dating for two months and really clicked; they laugh a lot, have fun, go kayaking, visit the zoo, and have romantic dinners. Unlike other men in Katie's past, Connor has texted her regularly and been attentive when they were together. So Katie is shocked when one night, while they are at a restaurant, Connor suddenly gets serious and tells her that things just aren't working out. Katie can't believe what she's hearing. She feels blindsided and thinks to herself, What happened? How could I have missed the warning signs?

Dr. Reef

In any relationship, there are obvious problematic warning signs, like not having much to talk about, not being able to see each other that much, having no physical or emotional intimacy, no attraction, etc. Someone may show attention, but deep down they may feel that the other person is not right for them. And then there are the *not-so-obvious* signs, like the other person isn't ready to have a relationship, or isn't over an ex, or is questioning his or her own sexual preference, or he or she just really likes the attention and validation but doesn't have the emotional-intimacy skills to be in a relationship. All you can do is take the journey.

Dr. Paula

First of all, Katie's got to stop beating herself up with the question, *How could I have missed the warning signs?* People end relationships for a lot of reasons. They don't feel chemistry. They don't have enough things in common with the other person. She wants kids, he doesn't. He's too materialistic, she's too career obsessed, etc., etc. Sometimes, it's hard to read all the clues.

Dr. Reef

Since we don't have the technology yet to figure out what the other person is thinking (unless you're a psychic, and even they have dating problems and end up in my office), you're usually not going to be aware of the really subtle warning signs until later in the relationship or until the other person tells you.

Dr. Paula

We can't avoid being blindsided in life. People who've been married for 30 years are sometimes blindsided when out of nowhere their spouse says, *"I'm not happy. I want a divorce."* If you spend a lot of time trying to predict what's going to happen, you won't get to enjoy what is happening in the here and now.

Dr. Paula: Your *"Move Forward or Move On?"* Self-Assessment

Emotional capital is finite and ultimately you'll want to decide if you should invest further in the relationship . . . or cut your losses. How do you know if the relationship is working for you? The way you answer the questions below will help you decide whether it's time to move forward — or to move on.

1) Are there any behaviors that make me think, *Well, it isn't a big deal now, but if he continues to do that in the future it could become a problem?* Examples are alcohol consumption or drug use.

2) Are there any red flags? Is his temperament something I can handle? Does he fly off the handle easily? How does he treat friends and family?

3) How do I feel about myself when I am with him? Am I at ease or am I insecure and uncomfortable?

4) Do I feel like I can be the "real" me? Can I imagine sharing something I'm ashamed of with him? Some examples include: *"I never got my college degree, but people think I have because I'm one class away." "I used to have a problem with drugs but haven't used in many years." "I got a DUI in college, and no one knows." "I was date-raped as a teenager." "I'm a real pack rat, and that's why we've never gone to my place."*

5) Are there profound differences in how we'd live our lives that would be close to insurmountable? For example: He wants to travel and live all around the world, taking a different job each year, while I want to throw down roots in one place and build a life there. Or he's a smoker and tells me he has no intention of quitting, while I am repulsed by cigarettes.

Cutting Your Losses or . . . ?

Over the past three months, Emily and Eric have been dating off and on, but for Emily the relationship has definitely felt more "off" than "on." When she first met him, she knew he had some "rough edges" (a more negative personality, and he's more introverted), but she thought those would change over time and that he'd come to want the same things she wants: to be closer as a couple and to think about a future together. Emily cares about Eric a lot, but lately she feels like she's had to make more compromises in her relationship with him than she's comfortable with. She's thinking of ending the relationship, but she's not sure if this is the right time. She wonders, Do I keep holding on, just in case he makes a turnaround, or do I hold off putting more effort into this relationship?

Dr. Paula

I'd say to Emily that it depends on what's happened so far. If things have been difficult for her from the get-go, then she has to ask herself how much more time and effort she's willing to invest. If she keeps thinking that Eric will "certainly change" as she continues dating him, but there's no evidence of it so far, then she has to consider that this is, in fact, unlikely. Don't date someone for who you hope he'll become. Look at who he is now.

Staying with someone in hopes that he'll change is not a great investment. The best predictor of future behavior is past behavior. It isn't your job to change him or "make him a better man."

Dr. Reef

Do you cut your losses or hang in there? I'd love to say there's an easy answer here, but there isn't. Each situation is different for each person. It depends how often you see him, how much time you've invested, what the compromises are, and what needs to change to make the relationship work. Idealizing someone and dating him for his potential usually doesn't work and often leaves you frustrated. People do change, but core characteristics of people usually don't. For example, a big-time cheater who's incredibly selfish will require a major life change, some good therapy, and a lot of maturity to change his ways.

Dr. Paula

Compromise is an important part of relationships and of life. It's how we grow. It isn't surprising that many extroverts hook up with introverts, or more optimistic people hook up with more negative types (though each person tends to see himself or herself as a realist, right?).

Compromise comes from a place of recognizing that to be in relationship with another person requires some degree of letting go of what you want in order to build a healthy relationship. A willingness to give in is an excellent quality to have for long-term success in relationships. But let's not confuse "giving in" with "giving up who you are."

Dr. Reef

Generally, if you have to change too much of yourself or compromise so much that you lose yourself in the process, then you may need to move on. Also, timing is such a huge factor in dating. You may have found the perfect person but not at the perfect time. Nobody wants to let that person go, but sometimes you need to let go to realize that this may not be the right person, or that this relationship may end up working out in the future, but not now. We can't force someone into a relationship. The tricky part, especially with guys, is that some guys need a little pressure to jump into a healthy relationship, and without that pressure, they often don't make that decision.

So, how do you know if the guy just needs a little pressure, or if the timing is off and he's not ready for a relationship? Over time, asking the right questions and finding out where he's at in his life and what he's looking for can make a big difference, because he might not bring it up in conversation on his own.

Dr. Paula

There are many times in relationships where you hit forks in the road. You wonder, *Which path do I take?* One of the most stressful parts of the early stages of relationships is trying to figure out if you should move forward or move on. By gaining more knowledge about yourself, evaluating how you feel, and knowing what you want, you'll be better equipped to know if a relationship is right for you.

Advice from Dr. Paula: *Five Reasons to Stay and Keep Trying*

No one is perfect. In every relationship there are going to be disagreements and issues. We all can be easily irritated and irritating. What are signs that putting in the effort in the early stages could be worth it in the long run?

1) If, most of the time you are together, you feel relaxed, comfortable, and are able to show the "real" you.

2) If tension does exist, it is clearly tied to a change in his life (i.e., losing a job, death of a friend or family member). If he's stressed and being short tempered with you, and that is a change from what you're used to, then there is a reason behind his behavior.

3) If you do argue, it rarely gets mean and personal. Everyone will, at some point, disagree and argue. Conflict in and of itself does not mean your relationship is doomed. It's a good sign if you have differences and are able to respectfully disagree, or if your conflict leads to resolution.

4) If you share common values and goals when it comes to having children, where you want to live, how you will spend money, your faith, etc.

5) If you realize that problems in the relationship seem to correlate with problems within yourself. Does he only seem like a jerk once a month? Is it around the time of your period? Is it possible that it's you and not him?

CHAPTER 4: Sex and Intimacy

It was difficult to decide where in this book the topic of sex should appear. It's a significant part of every phase of a couple's relationship, whether they've just met or have been together for years. There are so many questions about the subject. Should you sleep together early in the relationship, to see if you are sexually compatible before investing too much time or energy in the relationship? How important is sexual compatibility? If you aren't immediately attracted to someone, can an attraction grow with time? Sex is a wonderful opportunity to connect with a partner, release tension, and improve overall happiness and health. Many problems in the bedroom have less to do with sex and more to do with self-esteem, overall stress, and poor communication.

THE SEX FACTOR

Dr. Reef

Men and women are not just different in terms of anatomy, we are also different in terms of our brain structure, function, and overall behavior. We are wired differently and have different skills that were originally developed for evolutionary purposes, but are now often the subject of praise or complaint by the opposite sex.

Guys think about sex a lot. It's not all we think about, but it does come up frequently (sometimes at the worst possible times). A recent study from Ohio State University was published in the *Journal of Sex Research*, looking at this very topic: *How often do men and women think about sex?* And then to stack the deck, they only asked college students aged 18–25. The students had a counter that they had to click every time they thought about sex. You'd think a bunch of them would have thumb injuries or carpal tunnel syndrome after a couple of days. A one-word description of the average college guy's brain might be: sex, food, sex, sports, sex, class, sex, food, sex, sex, sex.

But that's not what they found. On average, this segment of the male population thought about sex 18.6 times a day, and the women thought about sex 9.9 times a day. And what was the biggest competitor for their thoughts? Food. Men thought about food almost 18 times a day, and women thought about food almost 15 times a day.

Conclusion: Men think about food as much as sex. And they think about a lot of other things besides food and sex. Sorry ladies, men are a little more complex than you thought.

Dr. Paula

Men figure out how to sexually satisfy themselves from a young age. They start masturbating younger, and they pretty much get off every time. Because of this, they are confident about how things work. Women, however, see their own bodies as much more of a mystery.

Dr. Reef

A guy reaching his sexual peak at 18 is like someone being given the keys to a Ferrari and not knowing how to drive. By the time he figures out how to be skilled and creative in the sex department, his sex drive is already on the decline. It's one of the biggest ironies of life.

Dr. Paula

So much of a woman's sexual pleasure comes from how she feels about herself. The better she knows herself and her body, the easier it will be for her to guide her partner. The more responsibility she takes for communicating what she wants — rather than assuming that it is his job to figure it out — the better.

Dr. Reef

Many women in their twenties report feeling sexual, but they don't always report feeling that comfortable with their bodies. Depending on their sexual history and overall disposition, some women in their twenties are more comfortable than others.

Women in their thirties are definitely more comfortable with their bodies, their sexual energy, and their ability to have an orgasm. They have more self-confidence. They know what they need. They're more willing to describe to a partner what they want. When women in their 30s or 40s date guys who are between 18 and 22, it's pretty obvious they want to take a ride in the Ferrari and don't care if it crashes and burns. Needless to say, that's not conducive to a long-term relationship.

Dr. Paula

Age does play a major factor. Women are the ones who get pregnant. So when the probability of that lessens, many women relax and are better able to enjoy sex. Their desire and ability to be more fully engaged in sex blossoms (and their uterus and breasts don't have to!). After one mom I know decided not to get pregnant again, she told me, *"Wow, sex is great now! I worried all these years, and now I don't even have to think about it anymore."*

The other side of the fertility coin is interesting. So many women I work with who are trying to get pregnant in their mid- to late 30s find their sex drive diminishes. Somehow, the pressure to get pregnant makes sex feel like work. And work isn't always fun. These women tell me that their male partners, who used to be all over them, seem to lose interest in sex when it becomes so goal oriented. The goal of orgasm isn't a problem; the goal of conceiving is a different story.

Dr. Reef

Whenever there's major pressure to have sex for a specific goal, it usually stirs up anxiety or a feeling of being controlled, or a feeling that it's work and not fun. And a woman's strong fertility drive can either be a bonding experience for men or a turnoff.

For men, the bonding process gets easier as they get older. As men age, they experience higher levels of the hormone oxytocin, which acts as a neurotransmitter in the brain and can be responsible for helping people to bond, trust, and form long-term relationships. At 18, guys are sexually robust; at 28, they have some relationship skills and a pretty strong sexual response; by 38, they're more likely to be in a committed relationship, with more oxytocin and less testosterone in their system; and by 48, they're more mellow and more connected to their wife or girlfriend (although that little blue pill has changed this a bit). "Settling down" is a combination of finding the right woman, developing relationship skills, and spending time to connect. Our biology tends to help things along.

Dr. Reef

Men may appear to have higher sex drives early on in the relationship, because they don't need the emotional familiarity with a woman to have sex with her.

Dr. Paula

Often, a woman needs to experience intimacy to become more sexual, whereas for a man the portal to intimacy is sex. This fundamental difference is the reason why porn appeals to men and romantic comedies appeal to women — they're the female's version of porn.

Dr. Reef

Lifetime Channel movies and *Sex and the City* may be women's porn, but it's absolute torture for most men. Men don't need the story. We just need the stimuli.

Dr. Paula

Fine — when *Sex and the City 14* comes out, I know who I *won't* be taking to the premiere!

Dr. Reef

Would hate to miss out on that one . . .

Men and women are turned on differently. Women, depending on their mood, hormonal cycle, and comfort level, could be turned on right away, but more often than not it takes time and requires more of an emotional connection; it requires a man to read not only the physical but also the emotional instruction manual.

The average guy, on the other hand, could be turned on by an attractive woman just saying hello. . . . . .

Dr. Paula

The other thing is that men often become affectionate *after* they feel aroused, whereas women usually need to feel affectionate *first* in order to get aroused.

Dr. Reef

Some men get affectionate after being aroused; others just get more aroused.

READY, SET, SEX

Dr. Paula

Most young men would be happy to get right into sex, and to have women go right for the main event. They need to understand that women tend to prefer a slower buildup. Oftentimes, men go straight for her erogenous zones, and they neglect the rest of her body. But for women (and men as well, if they try it), taking things more gradually can heighten the sexual experience. Not to be too crass here, but men, you might want to remember that in the bedroom, "beating around the bush" is not such a bad thing!

Dr. Reef

Because men and women have such different perspectives, there are many opportunities for misunderstanding. Some men think that women's arousal systems (how quickly they want to have sex) and their fetishes should be just like men's. Some women think guys should just take it slow, not focus so much on sex, and spend more time talking and being more emotionally intimate. Obviously, there are differences. Being able to understand the biological and emotional differences of the opposite sex helps you to be better in bed. Being good in bed is not about how powerful or in shape you are, it's about how well you understand your body and your partner's body and the sensuality of the moment.

Dr. Paula

In sexual activity, my advice to men is this: Don't go straight for the "zone." Approach sex with a gradual buildup. Going in for the kill can actually be a turnoff.

Dr. Reef

Foreplay puts a woman at ease. It increases the pleasure. It gives her time to relax and get aroused. And it helps him to become familiar with her body; your bodies are communicating to each other during foreplay.

When a guy learns to love foreplay, he becomes a really desirable sex partner. Foreplay builds anticipation, makes her feel at ease, slows down the process, and increases the intimacy.

Advice from Dr. Reef: *Road Map to Better Sex for Guys (but can be used by women, too)*

---

1) Ask directions if you get lost (don't be afraid to ask what turns her on).
2) Start on the smaller roads (back of the knees, neck, hair, feet) before getting on the highway.
3) "Warm up the engine" using oil, massage, lotions, fruit, whipped cream.
4) Take your car to the shop for regular maintenance (get tested, stay in shape).
5) Read the manual (research what turns on the opposite sex).
6) Spend time talking in the car before starting the trip (quality time to emotionally connect).

Dr. Paula

In my practice, I see women who say they have the urge to have sex on the first or second date, but then when they act on that they're often disappointed when things don't work out well. Just because you want to have sex right away doesn't always mean you should. You need to think a few steps ahead and consider what will be the consequences of your actions. If you sleep with someone too early on, is it going to cloud your perspective on how compatible you are? Are women confusing love with the chemical/hormonal rush they get from their own sexual response?

Dr. Reef

Sleeping with someone too early can be hormonally and emotionally confusing, unless you're just looking for sex and can overcome your biological tendencies to connect after sex.

Dr. Paula

If you have sex too early, trust me, it will weigh on you and cloud your perspective about the relationship.

Dr. Reef

Sex can happen any time in the dating process, but you have to be emotionally and physically prepared for it. I've known couples and friends that had sex on the first date and got married, but I've also seen friends and individuals in my practice that had one-night stands, and it was so awkward that they never called the woman again or returned her calls. That's because they were either drunk when it happened and acted impulsively without thinking, or didn't have enough of a connection with the woman to continue the relationship — not even for a second date. Things like commonality, trust, a sense of humor, and similar backgrounds all play into that feeling of "connectedness" that makes you want to meet up again, whether you had sex or not (unless the sex is super bad). Bottom line: Sex just adds more pressure if it happens too early.

Dr. Paula

I agree. When sex enters the picture too early, it can totally complicate things. Like Reef, I know of couples that had sex on the first date, and they subsequently got married and had a great relationship, and everything has worked out well. However, more often than not, the reason was because they had a commonality of shared interests — a mutual sense of humor, trust in one another, and good communication skills. They usually also had excellent conflict-resolution skills, so that even though they had sex early on in the relationship, they were mature enough to work through any problems that might come up. But for most couples who introduce sex too early, it ups the ante and forces things to happen much more quickly. It shakes up the system too soon, and often those relationships fizzle out because there wasn't enough time for the couple to become compatible. The more casual sex we have, the more we struggle with being able to integrate emotion and sexual response. Like a wise young woman told me, *The concept that love actually enhances sex is surprisingly true!*

Dr. Reef

If you want to get to know another person seriously, you need to grow that relationship over time.

Some women say they're more inclined to sleep with a guy right away if they don't care much about building a connection with him (*"I think he's hot, but I know it'll never go anywhere"*). There's no worry about being judged by him or trying to establish anything. So, because they don't care about being judged, they may go for it. But if a woman is actively having casual sex — hooking up for just the sexual connection — she will need to deprogram her desire for an emotional connection, which in women has been an innate need that usually accompanies sex. It's an evolutionary response that is oppositional to the concept of casual sex. It's also why some women develop feelings after having sex with a guy — casual or not.

The Cardinal Rule

Dr. Reef

Every guy knows the cardinal rule is that you never talk about sex, or even the possibility of having sex, when you're on a first or second date. If sex happens, it happens. If she ends up back at your place, fine. If you end up back at her place, fine. But don't talk about it unless there's a comfort level there, or she's been asking about it all night, or you've discussed a long-term relationship; otherwise, if you just want something casual, you might scare her off if you bring up the subject. Nobody wants to come across like they're easy or they're just into casual sex. Most people want it to just happen naturally.

Dr. Paula

This is not a cardinal rule for women, Reef. It sounds more like a rule for guys who want to make sure that their chances for sex increase if they don't bring up sex. Women don't want to think that their date is planning to "get some" tonight. On the other hand, it if just sort of happens and is spontaneous, that's very different. That feels great.

Dr. Reef

Most guys know what *could* happen, and they know that

women want it to feel spontaneous. So, whether a guy is specifically planning it or he's just going with the flow, he knows he can't keep talking about sex. He wants her to feel comfortable. The reality is that most guys will think about sex at some point during the date. Some guys will act on it, and others won't. If a guy is interested in something more long term, he's less likely to want to have sex with you right away.

Dr. Paula

That's true for a lot of women, too. They don't want to admit that the sex was intentional. But that's when problems occur. They don't use condoms because having one on hand is an admission they were planning it all along.

Dr. Reef

It's definitely a "be careful" sign when a guy wants to wait to have sex because he doesn't have a condom, and the woman opens her nightstand drawer that's full of different-size condoms in her bedroom.

If a woman meets a guy and he's looking only for down-and-dirty sex, this means he doesn't want to get emotionally intimate at that time. Primal sex is usually impulsive and raw, with crazy energy — but it doesn't usually create an emotional connection.

Dr. Paula

When the other person is just a sex buddy, you're going to worry less about what he wants and more about what you want. In that type of relationship, you're going to be more selfish. When there's the possibility that you're heading towards something more long term, your sexual relationship will be laced with intimacy and a sense of connection between the two of you.

Dr. Reef

Sex can be impulsive and lusty, but being prepared and thinking long term is important. Guys might rush into sex if they've been drinking (alcohol makes you more impulsive), or if they think the woman might change her mind. Alcohol can change the course of any potential relationship. It's better not to get hammered, so you can let the other person know who you really are instead of the drunken version of you, especially when you're at the beginning of a relationship. When a relationship is about to get physical, a couple should speak to each other about condoms. If a woman suddenly gets pregnant or someone gets herpes or chlamydia, that relationship just changed big time.

Dr. Paula

I agree. Before you have sex, there are three things that need to be discussed: STDs, birth control, and what to do in case of an unwanted pregnancy. If you don't feel comfortable talking about these three things with your date, don't have sex!

Unfortunately, studies are showing that people are becoming complacent about sexually transmitted diseases. Care enough about yourself to stay safe.

Advice from Dr. Paula: *He Has Condom Issues*

Sample Scripts That Could Save Your Life

Him: *I don't enjoy it as much with a condom.*

You: *Well, I can't enjoy myself if I'm worried about getting an STD or getting pregnant.*

Him: *It just doesn't feel as spontaneous if I wear a condom.*

You: *The more we practice putting it on, the better we'll be at it. Actually, let me put it on for you!*

Him: *I know I don't have any STDs; don't you trust me?*

You: *I do trust you, but it's important to me that I be protected. Actually, I care so much about you that I want us both to be protected.*

Him: *We've done it before without using protection.*

You: *I know, but that really wasn't good judgment on my part. We got lucky that nothing happened, but I'm not willing to take that risk again.*

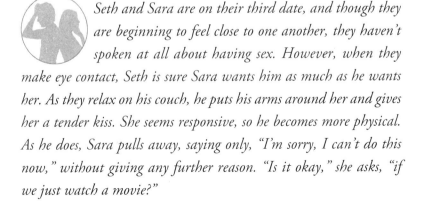

Seth and Sara are on their third date, and though they are beginning to feel close to one another, they haven't spoken at all about having sex. However, when they make eye contact, Seth is sure Sara wants him as much as he wants her. As they relax on his couch, he puts his arms around her and gives her a tender kiss. She seems responsive, so he becomes more physical. As he does, Sara pulls away, saying only, "I'm sorry, I can't do this now," without giving any further reason. "Is it okay," she asks, "if we just watch a movie?"

Dr. Paula

If Sara and Seth are connecting on a date but she pulls away from sexual intimacy, he may not perceive the situation correctly. He may not understand why she's not welcoming his bid for intimacy. To avoid confusion, she might say, *"Hey, you know, this feels really good. I like the way you're making me feel, but I'm not ready to go further right now."* That should be enough.

Dr. Reef

If she's not ready for sex and doesn't want Seth to take it as rejection, she needs to say *why* she's not ready. Otherwise, he's going to have no idea what's going on — particularly if things seemed good, and then there was an abrupt stop. If she indicates she's not in the mood, the first thing that goes through his mind is, *Why not? Is it something I said? Is it some kind of hormonal thing? What just happened?*

Dr. Paula

Or it could be that she has her period, or an STD, or she could be too high, too drunk, or maybe too sad. Reef, she might simply feel that it's too early to disclose these things.

Dr. Reef

Perhaps, but men are problem solvers, so they want to know the reason. They're thinking: *Is it something that I can help you with? Is it something I did? Is it because you like some other guy? Is it because I didn't manscape today? What is it?* Don't keep us in the dark.

Dr. Paula

First of all, in this scenario, if it's not any of the above, Sara has to know herself well enough to know what it is. Then she has to accept herself enough to have the courage to say that it's because she's not feeling good about herself, or that she's worried about her performance. Then, maybe, she and Seth can talk through the issues, and she can give him a chance to be there for her, instead of assuming he doesn't know how to hear her or support her.

Dr. Reef

Some women use the phrase *"I'm not really in the mood,"* but that brings up confusion, because men don't usually base their sexual response on their mood state. Men hate that expression, because it doesn't tell them anything. If a woman says *"I don't want to,"* with no explanation, the guy may take it personally and feel rejected. Share with us what's going on. If it's something personal that you don't want to discuss, then just say, *"I'm definitely attracted to you, and tonight was amazing and I'm excited to see you again, but I want to save something for later."*

Dr. Paula

The message I'm hearing from you, Reef, is that women have a lot of the power in a sexual relationship. Many men *want* to please women. I haven't had a single session with my female patients in the past month that didn't involve figuring out that it was okay for her to be in touch with her own body. It doesn't make her selfish. It's a very good investment in your relationship and your sex life to get to know yourself, whether it's physically, using a mirror as you masturbate, or checking in emotionally and asking yourself, *What's going on with me? Why am I so overwhelmed? Why is this sexual relationship freaking me out?* It's good to let men help you with that. Women don't give men a chance a lot of times, because they're scared that he's going to judge them. But a lot of times it's the woman who's judging herself.

Dr. Reef

Most men want nothing more than to see a woman sexually aroused and happy. But men have feelings too. If she doesn't reveal how she's really feeling, he may judge her based on very limited information. If women withhold information, it becomes a self-fulfilling prophecy.

In regard to sex, men are pretty simple. They either want it or they don't. Men often leave it up to her to decide when it's going to happen. All they ask is that she communicate.

Dr. Paula

Yes, and typically guys also leave it up to the woman to initiate any kind of discussion about sexual monogamy. But when she says that she wants to have a monogamous relationship, the guy often confuses it with a long-term commitment. If she wants to be exclusive, it doesn't mean she wants to pin him down forever. Guys immediately think, *Wait, wait, wait a second. Put on the brakes. How far along do you think we are?* They don't understand that women trust in their connections — that's what intimacy is for them. And the more connected they feel, the safer they feel — and the more they'll be willing to open up.

Dr. Reef

I think Paula's right — it is usually the woman who starts the exclusivity conversation. Men don't because they're either scared of commitment, aren't sure about the relationship, or want to keep their options open. Frankly, many guys get into an exclusive relationship because they don't want to see the woman with other guys. Men don't say to themselves, *We've been physically intimate, so now we should be exclusive.* No, most of the time it's about the man having her all to himself and not seeing her with other guys. Over time, the guy may get more emotionally intimate and then (hopefully) a stronger connection kicks in.

It's different if the guy is already emotionally connected to her and she brings up exclusivity; then he's much more likely to say, *"That's great. I've been thinking about a long-term relationship, too. Let's do it."* For some, monogamy is a precursor to a long-term relationship.

Dr. Paula

I recently had a session with a client, and she said to the guy she was dating, *"Listen, I cannot mess around with you if I know you're messing around with someone else. It doesn't mean I need an engagement ring, but if you really want to get to know me, then we've got to be exclusive. I appreciate your honesty in telling me you're seeing other women, but I can't become more intimate with you unless I know you're ready to be monogamous."* She was very clear with him about her boundaries and expectations.

Dr. Reef

But even if he agrees to be monogamous, she won't be sure *why* he's agreeing to it. The fact is, guys don't tell women their inner thoughts very often.

I've always felt that the power in a relationship is based on if and when there is an emotional connection. When the guy doesn't know how the woman really feels about him (usually when they first meet and early on), she has a little more of the power. Once he knows she's emotionally connected to him (after some time), then he has a little bit more of the power.

Ultimately, it all evens out.

Myths and Misperceptions

Dr. Reef

An important part of couples and relationship therapy is to understand that the way you look at things may not be the way the opposite sex sees them. When you need to actively listen and see what someone else's perspective is, it's called "crossing the perceptual line."

Dr. Paula

Speaking of differences and perception, you'd be surprised how common it is that men don't realize that the vaginal opening is not what is most stimulating for a woman. Men, my advice is to pick up a basic anatomy book and get a good look at what's down there. If you are currently in a sexual relationship and haven't seen her close up, then you might ask to do so. Pay particular attention to the clitoris. (Again, if you don't know where it is, look it up. No shame, just do the research!) Most women need clitoral stimulation to orgasm. What feels good to you guys, the in-and-out motion, is often not enough for a woman. It's just how she's designed.

Dr. Reef

Good transition.

The average guy does not understand all the intricacies of the mind/body connection. Guys are so used to the mechanics, the plumbing: if you do this and this, then that happens. It's a revelation for a lot of guys when I talk to them in my office about how psychological the whole process is. Guys want to please, but sometimes they need a road map (see page 106).

The research data shows that if a woman is feeling really safe and secure, and comfortable and open, and she's feeling good about what's happening, then it's going to be a lot easier to orgasm. Guys don't always realize this — as we said earlier, they assume the woman is just like them in regard to the mechanics of orgasm. Women need to feel comfortable. That's when the best sex occurs.

Dr. Paula

In order for that to happen, a man needs to be sensitive and attentive to a woman's needs. You know, I think it's a big misconception that men aren't sensitive. They are very sensitive. But the fact is, women still want men to be macho. They want a guy who's going to take charge, but at the same time they don't like the idea that they want a guy who's going to take charge. Of course, this is confusing as hell for everybody. She can't expect him to know that she wants him to take charge if she hasn't told him that. He may be scared of coming across as a macho asshole. You know what I mean? There has to be communication. What do you think, Reef?

Dr. Reef

I think two things are going on at the same time: Do many women want a sensitive guy who responds to her feelings? Yes. Do many women want a macho guy who will take charge and be great in bed? Yes. But those two attributes are often in opposition. For a guy to be both, he has to compartmentalize according to the situation, and that requires a lot of communication. It's also important for the guy to be who he is. Some guys are sensitive and others aren't. Generally, they want to take charge, but if they feel rejected or unappreciated, they'll stop trying.

If we're going to speak about men being sensitive, then I'd like to ask Paula to define what that is in our present time.

Dr. Paula

On the whole, I think our society has begun to have more of a comfort level with androgynous personalities. We've moved away from the outdated stereotype of "she's passive, he's domineering." It's not that he's powerful *or* he's sensitive. He's not one or the other — he's both. A guy can be a take-charge person *and* sensitive. We have to leave behind the kind of bifurcating black-and-white thinking that labels someone all this or all that, as if one is mutually exclusive from the other. It's the same for women. If I'm labeled "an independent woman" and then I act in a way that's needy, what do I do with that information? I freak out. I think, *Who am I?* It's not that I'm independent or needy — I can be both. We have to change the conjunction. We should be able to tolerate contradictions in each other. To acknowledge that we may be both at the same time. Change your conjunction, change your life.

Dr. Reef

I have specific opinions on this that may not be politically correct. I think the whole concept of androgyny is really bad. Women and men should be able to be whatever they want to be. But if we play the theme that "we're all the same," and ignore our biological, emotional, and evolutionary differences, that's going to hurt our relationship connections. We are different for a reason. Children do best with a mother and a father, and the specific strengths that go along with being male and female. We're not the same, and I don't believe we should be.

Dr. Paula

(taking deep breath, counting to ten before responding) Reef, there are times when professionals have differences of opinion, and I couldn't disagree more with what you've just said. In my experience, when you talk about the health and happiness of children, what matters most is that they have loving parents. Gender is irrelevant. Now, getting back to our discussion about how women want a take-charge guy who's also sensitive, I see a lot of women in my practice who are in their twenties, and they complain that guys aren't as sensitive to their feelings as they'd like them to be. She will say to him, *"I'm very upset about something that happened at work today,"* and she'll describe the issue in detail, and then he'll reply, *"Really? That doesn't seem like such a big deal to me."* Another woman will say, *"I lost out on a big promotion at work, and it didn't occur to my boyfriend to come over to my apartment to give me a hug."* Women want men to "get" them, to see the world through their eyes — but it rarely happens.

Dr. Reef

Of course, guys don't see the world the same way women do. Our emotional makeup is different. We don't think like you do. But on the other hand, we've been socialized in the last decade to be "the sensitive man." So when women complain, *"Why doesn't he take charge? Why doesn't he man up and plan a date?"* that's the reason. You're losing us on both ends. We're less powerful, and at the same time we're not biologically or environmentally geared to have your level of sensitivity. We don't want to be women. We like being guys. I'm not saying we should be cavemen, but we should be different from you. We should not be androgynous; we should not be the same. I think a healthy relationship is one where the man and woman are different, and they work well together synergistically.

Dr. Paula

I don't think we should push men to be androgynous. What I'm saying is that because we aren't bound so much by the old traditional roles, it's now roomier to be a man. It's now roomier to be a woman. Many guys are still "guy guys," but there are other men who have more nuanced personalities, and there's room for that, too. Before, they were pushed into a corner. For example, there was a time when men weren't supposed to express sadness — they had to hold it all in. It's more socially acceptable for people to be more fully themselves. It goes back to knowing who you are so you can explain what it is you need. And it means that a woman shouldn't just automatically assume that if she's crying and her boyfriend doesn't give her a hug, that he's a jerk.

Dr. Reef

But there seems to be a trend toward viewing men as more primal and women as more evolved — and I just don't buy that. Men have feelings, but because we are historically quicker to take action, less risk averse, and generally more sexually assertive, we get a bad rap.

Men also get a bad rap for being so easily distracted by sexual stimuli; it's often true that men can't think about anything else when they're focused on sex. That's why 25 hot-and-bothered guys who were screaming and playing football two minutes earlier will not utter a sound while watching porno at a bachelor party.

Here's another interesting misperception exposed: a recent Kinsey study on relationships and sex reported that men actually like "cuddling" a little more than women. And their research revealed that sexual satisfaction in a long-term relationship was actually more important to women than men. The "big reveal" from this study is that men do like "cuddling" and "affection" but they don't like talking about it, and women definitely want sexual satisfaction.

Dr. Paula

Wow! We have so many similar core needs, but they're fulfilled so differently. I think one of the biggest misperceptions in sex is that if *he* likes it, then *she'll* like it. If he likes it fast, then she likes it fast. If he needs it daily, then she needs it daily. When there is a difference between what he wants and what she wants, women will often think there is something wrong with them.

What Women Want vs. What Women Think They Want

Dr. Paula

Reef, tell me the truth. How does a guy really feel about a woman if she has sex with him on the first date?

Dr. Reef

Here are the first three questions he's going to ask himself:

1) *How good was the sex?*
2) *What do I know about her?*
3) *What are the chances she's doing this with other guys?*

He may categorize her as a "fun but don't take her seriously" type of girl if he thinks she does this with a bunch of other guys.

Dr. Paula

So, in terms of the *"How good was the sex?"* question: How much impact does the answer have on a man's decision whether to call her back?

Dr. Reef

It has a great impact. Sex feels good. So, most guys would call back hoping to have sex again. Then, if he happens to get to know her along the way, there may be hope for something more than just sex. It doesn't take a rocket scientist to figure out that he will call her again if he liked the sex. What's important is that she understands that it might be only about the sex, especially if there isn't any other connection, so she shouldn't necessarily get her hopes up for something more.

Dr. Paula

So, if the sex is awesome, is it possible it would make a guy want to date her?

Dr. Reef

It would make him want to see her again. That's it. What it doesn't mean is that it will necessarily lead to any kind of relationship.

Dr. Paula

Do you think a guy makes a decision really quickly when he first meets a woman about whether she's "girlfriend" material or if they're just going to be "friends with benefits"?

Dr. Reef

Most of the time it's not really about her. It's about where he is in his life. For some men, the date can be the sexiest and most amazing woman in bed, and have everything he's looking for, but she may still end up in the "friends with benefits" category because he's not ready to be a boyfriend to anyone.

Dr. Paula

Okay girls, hear that? It's him, not you. Stop wasting your time and investing too much in a situation if you haven't progressed to girlfriend (unless, of course, you aren't any more ready to have a relationship than he is). If you want a committed relationship, you are not going to get it by being a friend with benefits.

Dr. Reef

Or by "hanging out."

Hanging Out vs. Friends with Benefits

Dr. Paula

I think "hanging out" is just another way of saying you're physically involved with someone for whom commitment is low on the priority list. It's not really dating. It's a euphemism for the "benefits" part of a "friends with benefits" relationship.

Dr. Reef

I think "friends with benefits" is more of a commitment than "hanging out."

Dr. Paula

Really?

Dr. Reef

Yes. In a "friends with benefits" situation, the couple goes to the movies together and does some of the fun stuff that couples do — but they don't commit to each other in regard to having a relationship. They have a great physical relationship and they really enjoy each other's company, but they're not ready to be exclusive.

However, in a situation where a guy joins his friends at a bar or club and sees the woman he's been "hanging out" with, they are likely to talk to friends, get drinks, and possibly end up at his or her place to mess around, but they're not a couple and they're not friends with benefits, they're just conveniently there with each other.

Dr. Paula

I see it so differently. My feeling about the whole "friends with benefits" thing is that you've basically decided that the other person is *not* somebody you want to date, but you really like him and you have sex on a regular basis. In this kind of relationship, each of you can even talk about what's going on in your dating life, and you support each other through the ups and downs of those dates. The assumption is usually that once the person becomes exclusive with someone else, you'll stop having sex with him. I thought hanging out was a pretty similar situation.

Dr. Reef

Hanging out is not as much of a steady thing as friends with benefits. Hanging out is lazy.

If I'm with her at the end of the night, I might take her home.

I see a lot more people who are friends with benefits suddenly become more involved. It sneaks up on you, because you truly enjoy their company. (Ask Ashton Kutcher or Justin Timberlake.) I agree that friends with benefits implies that you aren't going to get serious about this person, but feelings have a funny way of surfacing between men and women over time . . . especially if they're both single.

Dr. Paula

Reef, I don't know if I agree with you. Maybe it's semantics. The women I see talk about hanging out as a way to start a relationship with a guy. They say, *"I really like this guy, but I don't want to overwhelm him, so we're not dating, we're just kind of hanging out."* But the fact is, a lot of times the women are really interested in the guy and want a relationship. Some see it as a slow buildup to a relationship that gives them the time to decide if they want to get into a relationship that way, beyond hanging out. It's a broad, roomy kind of thing, the way my clients are experiencing it.

Dr. Reef

When people in their twenties and thirties talk about hanging out, they usually assume that neither of them, at that time, is looking for a long-term relationship.

Dr. Paula

So, hanging out is sort of like texting, right? It's relatively innocuous.

Dr. Reef

Yes, that's *why* they're hanging out. They are looking for something less invasive than friends with benefits. They just want to hang out (usually in a group) rather than as a couple. Or they just use the expression "hang out" to make it clear that it's not a relationship. That's very different from someone who's seeking a long-term relationship.

 Kristen and Simon met through mutual friends while both were out at a club. They flirted and had an instant attraction, and one thing soon led to another. On weekends, they usually hang out together with their friends, playing pool and making each other laugh. They're careful not to let the others in their group know what's going on. Kristen likes Simon and feels that sex with him is hot, but she's not sure where things are going. She tells her best friend, "I'm tired of pretending in front of the group that nothing's going on between me and Simon. There's something exciting about the secretiveness of it all, but now I'm starting to resent the fact that I feel like I can't ask him for something

more. That all we're doing is just hanging out . . ."

Dr. Paula

Kristen has to understand that if she's hanging out with Simon, but she really wants a relationship that's deeper and more exclusive, she's going to get more and more frustrated and irritated. I think it's important for her to have clarity. Here's the point I want to emphasize, Reef. If a guy's just hanging out with a woman, playing video games or drinking beers with her and other friends, it probably means that he likes her company — but that he's not looking for more at this time.

Dr. Reef

Simon may not want a relationship with Kristen, or he may be open to a relationship with her if he knows she wants it, too, or he may not want a relationship with anyone. It's hard to know what he's thinking without getting more information from him. But one thing is for sure. If he feels comfortable knowing that every Saturday night he's going to see Kristen, and there's a good chance they'll go home together and fool around or have sex, then he has no incentive to look for anything more. He'll probably be content with the current situation, unless it changes or he really desires a long-term relationship. With just "hanging out," there are no defined rules. It's the Wild West of dating. You're not really dating; there are no strings attached and no expectations, but there is comfort and familiarity with that person. *"Hey look, we ended up back at your place again . . . how does that keep happening?"*

Dr. Paula

Sometimes, women like Kristen find this situation very difficult because it is so ambiguous.

Dr. Reef

If you're a guy who's not looking for a long-term relationship, hanging out is nirvana, because you get to flirt with a woman, have a good time with her, make out with her if it leads to that, have sex with her if it leads to that, and not worry about any major pressure of doing anything more because the boundaries of the "relationship" haven't been defined. You didn't say you were dating her.

Dr. Paula

So if Kristen wants a long-term relationship, she's going to need to articulate what she wants. Simon's going to assume she's okay with the status quo unless she tells him otherwise.

Dr. Reef

Exactly. If you're a woman and you're looking to just hang out, then great, have at it. But if you're actually looking for a long-term relationship, at some point you're going to have to put that out there. If he doesn't want more of a commitment, then your relationship's going to die an early death. I'd say 25 percent of the time, he actually wanted something more long term — and was just waiting for her to say something.

Dr. Paula

If a woman's in this situation, she's got to be honest with herself — and with him. If she says she wants something long term and he says, *"Listen, I'm just happy hanging out,"* she'll need to make the decision whether it's time to move on. That's the empowering part for a woman.

FAKING IT

Dr. Paula

There's a lot of faking going on among women, whether it's an orgasm or pretending to be happy. Why? Because it's easier to fake it than it is to ask a man to please you. I've seen estimates that anywhere between 50 to 70 percent of women have faked orgasm. Isn't that a terrible number?

Dr. Reef

Paula, 50–70 percent is such a high number. The crazy part is that most guys have no clue when a woman's faking it.

Dr. Paula

Women fake a lot of things because it's in their nature to keep their loved ones happy. In this case she may worry about how long it's going to take her to climax, and faking it seems like the best option. And that's too bad. In this case, it's a missed opportunity to have some fun and feel really good. The less you care about yourself and your needs, the more you're going to be faking things like orgasms.

Here are a few of the main reasons women fake it:

- She doesn't want to hurt his feelings
- She is tired and just wants it to be over
- She's self-conscious that she is taking too long
- She's never had an orgasm and she's ashamed

What women need to do is to concentrate more on their own needs and to communicate them to their partner. When women give men feedback, my advice is: don't take it personally. She isn't criticizing, just offering pointers.

Discussions about what you don't like doing while having sex should be held outside the bedroom. Keep bedroom talk positive and reassuring.

Dr. Reef

Communicating is a challenge for guys as well. When it comes to sex, they sometimes have difficulty asking for what they want, especially if it might be considered bad or kinky or hurtful to the other person. I have patients who tell me that they have sex for hours but they don't orgasm. Nothing happens. The fit's not there and they don't feel comfortable saying something — so they get frustrated and just give up. You know, men have these protective feelings towards women. They don't want to disappoint or hurt a woman's feelings by not having an orgasm, but they don't always know how to talk about what they need. Men and women are not that different in this regard, even though the mechanics are different.

Dr. Paula: *Breaking the News That You've Been Faking It*

Jacquie had had enough. She thought Dean was hot, but when they had sex he always seemed to lose interest after he had his orgasm. Usually, she'd fake an orgasm so he'd be happy, but she felt he was really clueless about what he needed to do to satisfy her. One night, after he had rolled over to his side of the bed, she just tersely blurted out, "I've been faking it. Not just tonight, but lots of other nights, too. I just feel like you're in a race to get to the finish line and you're not even interested in how I feel."

If you've been faking orgasm, stop in the name of sexual satisfaction! The first step is to be honest with your guy. If you don't tell him, he'll think that what he's doing is working. Of course, nothing can crush a guy's ego more quickly than this naked truth. In the scenario above, instead of blurting out the truth, Jacquie should begin with a gentle lead-in:

"I really want us both to have as much excitement as possible when we're together. . . ."

With any luck, Dean will agree, which will get both of them on the same page up front. Then she can continue. She should let him know that, even though the reason has to do with his technique, she hasn't communicated with him as well as she should have. Here's a possible script Jacquie could use:

"I haven't always been able to reach orgasm, because you seem to be in such a rush. I'm really sorry I didn't tell you earlier. But I feel we can trust each other enough so that it would be okay for

me to tell you this."

Now that she's said this, Jacquie can begin to explain what she needs to solve the problem:

"It takes me much longer to orgasm than it does you. Sometimes, I feel like you might be getting impatient."

Often we make assumptions that just aren't accurate, so Jacquie will want to follow this up by saying:

"Are you okay with it taking me however long it takes?"

Finally, Jacquie can ask Dean if it's okay to give him feedback during sex:

"Is it okay if I let you know what works for me and what doesn't?"

If you've never had an orgasm, tell him this is the case, and then discuss what you'd like to do with him — and what you're doing on your own — to try to learn to have one. As you speak, reassure him that this is not his fault. With this sample script, you'll hopefully be able to go from faking it to making it happen.

. . . But Who's Counting?

Melanie was having lunch with her girlfriends when the subject of how many times each of them was having sex with their boyfriends came up. "Well?" Laura asked, turning to Melanie, who was the last to speak up. "What about you and Adam?" Melanie could feel her face turn hot and flushed. Everyone else had talked about doing it three or four times a week, and she and Adam were usually content with just once a week or much less. She wondered, Is there some magical number that's right? How many times a week should we be doing it?

Dr. Paula

"Shoulds" get people in trouble. This is why I often tell my clients to "stop 'shoulding' all over yourself." Stop asking, "Am I having enough sex? Am I having too much sex?" I'd say to Melanie, *"Don't worry about what everybody else is doing. You're having enough sex if that's what works for you and Adam. What matters is, are you happy with the number of times that you are having sex?"* Comparing yourself to some sort of concept of how it should be only gets people into trouble. Who cares what anyone else is doing? The only time it's useful to have a sense of the norm is when you're doubting yourself and asking, *Am I crazy to feel like I could have sex more?*

Dr. Reef

There's no magical number when it comes to having sex in a relationship, although once every five years or ten times a day probably means there's a problem. The bottom line is that as long as both people are happy, that's what counts. Couples get in trouble when one person always wants sex and the other one doesn't. Every couple is different, and every person is different. Some people need sex every day, some people like Melanie and Adam are happy having sex once a week, some people need it once a month, and some people need it a few times a year. Sex is definitely important in a relationship, but there are also many other components to a healthy relationship.

Dr. Paula

Sometimes as the relationship progresses, you may not always make time for the sexual relationship. A couple may need to become more deliberate and plan an intimate evening together. It's a matter of action preceding motivation. Sometimes you need to fall back on that when the feelings aren't as easily accessible because you've fallen into the habit of a daily routine.

People will often say that making an appointment to get together sexually is not spontaneous enough. Well, my response is: how long has it been since you've had sex? Sometimes you have to schedule it. You don't always need to wait to feel like having sex in order to actually have sex. However, once you start, you might really get into it, even if at first you didn't feel up to it. It's not like you always have to coordinate your iCal or Outlook calendars. But when you're finding that things are slowing down, you need to evaluate to see why and what you can do about it.

I hear couples in my practice say, *"We used to feel like doing it all the time, and now we don't."* So the question is: What were you doing back then? Often people respond: *"We were watching less TV, hanging out more, leaving the laptops at the office, turning our phones off. We were connecting more.* "Well then, there you go.

Dr. Reef

Sometimes, the sex is given lower priority over the course of the relationship, and other times a couple experiences uneven sexual drives. I can't tell you the number of times I've seen patients in relationship therapy who are at different places sexually. He may be so focused on work that he's not sexually aroused very often, even though she is. Or she may be worried about something and not be interested in sex. One of my male patients said, *"We were having a great night. Everything was fantastic. We were just about to have sex, and then she completely changed. The fun disappeared; it just stopped. What happened?"* This couple had an unresolved conflict from earlier that day that was still bothering her, and she couldn't have sex until it was worked out.

Dr. Paula

When a couple has uneven sex drives, the first thing they should do is acknowledge it, and know that men *and* women tend to take any hint of a problem in the sexual arena very personally.

Dr. Reef

That's right. Most guys can have an orgasm. And we genuinely want to help a woman have one as well. But if the guy doesn't understand how to make that happen or it's taking a long time, he'll think he's doing something wrong and get frustrated.

Dr. Paula

If he says *"I'm not in the mood,"* she might interpret that as, *"You're not attractive. Your ass is too big."* More often, one person's lower sex drive is not about his or her partner, it's about him- or herself. It's important to make sure that you're not overthinking it, and one way to do that is to talk to your partner about what's going on. These are really good conversations to have outside of the bedroom. Positive interactions and conversations — like telling your partner what you like — belong *in* the bedroom. However, as previously discussed, a conversation about what you don't like is better discussed in a different place. Keep the bedroom as a place for relaxation and pleasure. Don't let it be associated with criticism or negativity.

Dr. Reef

Yes, like Paula said, there are good places for conversation and there are not-so-good places for conversation. The difficult part is if you care about someone, you want to *talk* to her and make her feel better. While you're actively trying to have sex is usually not the best time to throw out criticism.

For example, this is *not* a productive conversation:

Man: *How's that, baby, you like that?*
Woman: *Ow, that hurts.*
Man: *What do you mean, 'that hurts'? I'm barely touching you.*
Woman: *What's wrong with you? You don't have one sensual bone in your body.*
Man: *You know that's not true — I got at least one.*
Woman: *You're an idiot, you know nothing about foreplay, and you're bad in bed.*

Nothing good will come out of this conversation. Talking about or showing what feels good with positive commentary (no name calling and no ignoring the problem) would be a much healthier way of communicating.

Dr. Paula

I agree. And when situations come up where one person's sex drive is not as strong, you don't want to criticize. Instead, it's good to remember what was mentioned earlier: action precedes motivation. Sometimes, you don't feel sexual until you're actually having sex. There's this idea that you always have to feel inspired to do things; well, when you're in a long-term relationship or you're married, that's a load of crap. It is not so different than going to the gym. A lot of times you just don't feel like getting your butt to a workout, but once you've done it, you almost always feel better.

Dr. Reef

Not all men have high sex drives. There might be nothing wrong with the guy, or maybe he doesn't have as much testosterone or he's more focused on work or wants affection and isn't as sexual. Or he may simply get tired after his orgasm and run out of steam. It's not an ideal situation, but it happens sometimes. I've seen this happen with a lot of couples — the relationship is fine, it's just that his sex drive is not as high as hers.

This is a problem because she may feel rejected, he may feel inadequate, and nobody's happy. Until they talk about it. Some men complain that they have to be mind readers when they're with a woman. Men don't share the same level of emotionality that women have. People say, *"Oh, well, women are much more in touch with their emotions or much more together because they're emotional."* I don't necessarily agree with that. I think men need to understand the mind/body connection better and be more emotionally connected, but I also think women experience so much emotional stimuli that it can overwhelm their system. There needs to be improvement on both sides.

Dr. Paula

I agree, there needs to be a balance. A woman was sharing that she had gained ten pounds in the last year, and she went from feeling really good in her body to feeling bloated and wanting to have sex with the lights off. It became a real issue for her, because eye contact was very important to her sense of connection and therefore her ability to have an orgasm. When she asked her partner about how he felt about her body, he said he hadn't really noticed (which was, by the way, the right answer).

Dr. Reef

Women might not want to say, *"I feel bloated,"* but they could say, *"I'm not feeling sexy right now."* We would accept that because it gives us information (although we may try to convince you how sexy you actually are).

Men need to understand how potentially fragile a sexual connection really is. If there's a deep emotional connection, there usually isn't a ton of pressure on the couple to have "perfect sex." With a good connection, there will be more communication, and you can laugh about things and enjoy the whole experience. If there's not much of an emotional connection, sex can be pressure filled or impulsive or can cause major stress.

Mechanically and psychologically, when men and women are nervous or self-conscious, they can have a harder time performing or reaching orgasm. If a woman is nervous about the sexual experience, she's going to have a more difficult time having an orgasm. If she's having a bad day, or if there's something else that's taking up space in her head, it's going to have an impact on her. This might be why many people have a cocktail before having sex. In a good relationship, the couple often finds healthier ways to shift from the stresses of daily life to the bedroom.

"Houston, We Have a Problem"

Dr. Reef

Male impotence (not getting it up) is primarily psychological. We're not these primal creatures that just go-go-go. It's true that men are usually more comfortable with sex earlier in a relationship than women are (sometimes within minutes of meeting someone). But guys aren't always 24/7 ready for sex. Sometimes men are thinking about work, or they're nervous about a meeting or thinking about something else (even men think about their imperfections). Men definitely have insecurities about their bodies, and more and more are suffering from body dysmorphic disorders.

If a man can't get an erection, he's going to take it personally. As you mentioned earlier, Paula, everyone takes sexual problems personally. And she's going to think that he's not turned on by her. This happened to one of my patients. He was a virile, young man, but one night he experienced "failure to launch," and that single event was humiliating. It became all he thought about every time he met someone new.

In order to help him, I initially did some cognitive behavioral work with him to discover what was triggering those negative thoughts. Was it seeing a woman naked? He said no. Was it kissing? No again. What was it, then? He responded, *"When she's lying on the bed and I'm there and I'm about to orgasm, I can't. I lose my erection for a second and become anxious, and I start flashing back. I start re-experiencing that feeling of being impotent, and I go through the experience again in my mind, and eventually it just wipes me out and I can't do it."*

I asked him to see what would happen if he asked her to masturbate in front of him using a vibrator. When he did that, he saw she was getting turned on, he became aroused, and then he traded places with the vibrator and it all worked out fine. And from then on, he carried a vibrator with him. It became a security blanket. He knew if ever he couldn't do it, he'd just use the vibrator. And that helped him so much that eventually, he didn't need it.

Dr. Paula

When it comes to vibrators, I say, *"Boys, don't fear the toys!"* But it is true that women sometimes become too dependent on the vibrator and kind of desensitized from the degree of vibration and are not able to get off when there's somebody else in the room. Do you see that in your practice, Reef?

Dr. Reef

Absolutely. There was one couple where the woman was "addicted" to her vibrator. Her boyfriend just couldn't match up — and he couldn't handle it because she was so used to a certain vibrational sensation. He began to feel very threatened by it.

The more that you think about sexual problems happening, the more there's a chance they're going to happen. I think that most women don't realize that men definitely have performance anxiety, especially early on in the dating process. That's why a lot of men try to orgasm quickly — so they don't screw it up. They don't want anything to change in the moment. Some guys will drink to try to counteract the anxiety and overcome it, but that causes its own potential impotency issues.

Also, sometimes early on in a relationship, especially when the couple doesn't know each other well, a woman may have second thoughts about having sex, based on what she's feeling. It's very different for men. When a man is close to orgasm, he's going, going, gone. He doesn't want anything to interrupt that.

That's another reason a man wants to seize the moment, before he says the wrong thing, or her phone rings and her best friend says she just broke up with her boyfriend, or something happens externally that can influence the sexual connection — there's lots of things that might happen that can change a woman's desire. Guys tend to get on autopilot.

Now, it's completely different when the relationship is already established and the couple has more of a comfort level. The guy feels safer. The woman feels safer. There's a track record. He's not worried if there happens to be a performance problem one night. It's not as big of a deal because he knows — and she knows — that he's done it well a lot of other times before. And she might actually help him through it, as opposed to the situation being awkward and the woman making him feel like he's inadequate because he wasn't able to finish. In a longer-term relationship, the man (and woman) feels much more of a sense of trust.

Dr. Paula

Another common and highly treatable area of sexual dysfunction in men is premature ejaculation. All young boys are premature ejaculators. Over time, they get better at controlling their orgasms. What is it? Basically, ejaculation is premature if it happens before you or your partner want it to. If a guy comes after six minutes, it isn't premature ejaculation if she has an orgasm after only four minutes.

There are tons of resources online to give you information about a variety of useful strategies and techniques. What's important is that you are able to be open about it. Men, realize that it can be very frustrating for women (remember what we said earlier about the amount of time she needs in order to orgasm). Ladies, be supportive and compassionate. He's not doing it on purpose.

Advice from Dr. Paula: *How to Help Your Partner
Deal with Premature Ejaculation*

---

1) Recognize that he may be embarrassed and not want to discuss it with you. Let him know that you want to help and are willing to support him in any way. If he doesn't want to talk about it the first time, be patient and bring it up again.

2) Let him know how it affects you. For example, you can say: *"I really like the feeling of having you inside me, and when you come quickly I feel frustrated and disappointed."* Let him know that it isn't him you are disappointed with but rather the action. Let him know that you understand that it isn't his fault by saying, *"I imagine that this is frustrating for you as well. Let's figure out how to work on this together."*

3) Suggest that there are other ways, besides intercourse, that can satisfy you. Perhaps he can help you achieve orgasm through oral or manual stimulation first, and then that takes the pressure off. Let him know that you don't need to have an orgasm each time — but only say this if it's true!

4) Find information online about the high cure rates and different ways to treat premature ejaculation. Many times, you don't even need to see a professional.

5) If self-help strategies aren't working, encourage him to find a sex therapist. Tell him that you'll be as involved as he wants. Offer to help him find the therapist or schedule an appointment, and even attend it with him if he wants. But understand, there are men who will not want you to be involved in any manner.

Dr. Reef

Premature ejaculation is not something guys plan to do. It's not like they're thinking, *I can't wait to have sex with her for three-and-a-half amazing minutes, disappoint her, feel like a loser, and then go home.*

Sometimes, it happens because men are anxious and need to get it over with quickly. Sometimes it happens because the man doesn't understand his own body yet or hasn't yet developed his start/stop skills sufficiently.

The key treatment: foreplay. The more the man can focus on sensuality and foreplay and learn to calibrate the pressure, the better. He needs to learn how to pace himself. Use the start/stop method. Practice. Practice. Practice.

Dr. Paula

That's right, Reef. And as I mentioned earlier, of all sexual problems, premature ejaculation is by far the most treatable. It has close to a 100 percent cure rate!

Dr. Reef

Yes, and that's why it's important for men to develop their start/stop skills. For women, the best lovers are men that can summon a raw, primal kind of energy, and then are able to hit the "pause" button for a while and focus on different areas of her body — her neck, her knees, her thighs, her shoulders, exploring the nerve endings and being creative — and when it's all good, they hit the "play" button again.

The best sex is a combination of feeling comfortable and connected mixed with a sense of spontaneity, of doing something new to keep the relationship fresh, whether it's using sex toys or going to a new place or creating some sense of novelty. And when it's early on in a relationship, you can have the novelty, but the couple may not yet feel connected or comfortable. You have to build toward that sense of intimacy and comfort to get to the place where it'll be ideal.

Porn: Pleasure or Problem?

Dr. Reef

Porn can help a relationship or it can hurt it, depending on how it's used. It can help if it stimulates the couple's sexual feelings or gives them a few ideas that they can try out. But it can hurt if it causes a guy to objectify women to such an extent that he can't have a fulfilling relationship with a real woman; he gets lost in the fantasy world as opposed to the reality of what a woman in his world can do.

I was doing relationship therapy with this guy and his girlfriend, and he got really frustrated and yelled at her, *"Why can't you be more like Nikki?"* So I asked, *"Who's Nikki?"* And his girlfriend said, *"That's the name of the porn actress he watches every night before he goes to sleep."* That's definitely not a good sign.

Dr. Paula

Whether it's a man viewing it or a woman, porn use becomes a problem when it negatively affects someone's functioning or daily living.

Dr. Reef

There's no cardinal rule. It's based on functionality. You could watch porn for three hours a day, but still be able to do everything in your life, and you're fine. Or you can watch just every now and then, but it screws up your entire relationship.

There are a few red flags, however, like masturbating until you have physical problems, or become so obsessed with sex that you can't think about anything else. If you watch porn nonstop and stop interacting with real people, that's a bad sign.

Porn is all about visual stimulation, and as we've discussed, men are very visual. Porn also features women who are totally uninhibited, and this is a big-turn on for men. They are watching women who'll do *anything,* who'll act out a man's craziest fantasies, plus they don't hear them say "no." They can imagine anything happening, without that whole filter of, *Will my wife do this?* or *Can I ask my girlfriend to do this or will she think I'm crazy?* Guys are used to hearing "no" quite a bit, especially early on in the relationship. If a man doesn't have a steady girlfriend or wife or someone else who can be adventurous with him, he may just fantasize using porn.

It's interesting to note that more and more women are viewing porn; it's because of easy access and anonymity. I've treated a few women for porn addiction.

Dr. Paula
But even though more women are watching it, there are other women who simply find porn offensive and objectifying and no amount of understanding why men use it will help them to feel more comfortable with it.

Throughout life, people grow physically, spiritually, and emotionally. It's not uncommon for an interest in porn to diminish as one gains greater fulfillment from one's relationships, career, and hobbies. Emotional maturity often means outgrowing things like porn and excessive alcohol or drugs. For many, maturity inspires a desire to connect more deeply with life. Why use things to distract you, when life itself is so stimulating?

Dr. Reef

Sometimes people use porn to alter their mood or medicate symptoms like depression, anxiety, guilt, and shame. And if it gets really bad, it could be diagnosed as a hypersexual disorder or a compulsive sexual behavior problem. I treat a lot of sex addiction, and it can present in many different ways: problems related to trauma, impulse control, obsessive thinking, drugs and alcohol, etc. Often, people get lost in a fantasy world. Sexually acting out is a way of escaping, numbing, or distracting one's self. However, only a small percentage of the people who view porn have serious problems controlling their behavior. The porn often elicits insecurity by way of comparison (usually by the woman) or by occupying sexual interest (usually in the man).

Dr. Paula

People don't necessarily have to have full-on depression to have a problem with porn, just like you don't have to be a full-on alcoholic to maybe use a little too much alcohol to deal with your mood. You don't have to be an addict to notice, *When I'm stressed out, I download more porn.* It can be a useful barometer of what's going on in your life.

If you really think it's a bad thing that he's looking at porn, you have to look at your own self and see what it's about for you. Are you feeling threatened because the women he's looking at don't look like you? Are you worried that he's not as into you? This is something you need to admit to him and discuss. If you feel very strongly about it, it may be a deal breaker for you.

Like Reef said earlier, there are many women who enjoy porn, too, but the more common complaint is from women who don't want their men watching porn. These women often feel "less than," like they're being compared to the women in porn movies, and they think to themselves, *If he's turned on by this blonde with big boobs and fake nails, then it's impossible for him to genuinely be turned on by me, a brunette who got her last manicure for her high school prom.* This is a false assumption. Going back to what Reef said, a lot of times, arousal is just a conditioned response for men. It's not personally about her and her characteristics. Part of the problem for women is that they compare themselves and feel they've fallen short. It becomes a big rejection, as if he was having an affair with another woman.

Dr. Reef

I had a couple come in for therapy, and she gave him the ultimatum, *"Either the porn goes or I do."* I asked her, *"Why? How could porn have as much power as a real human being?"* One of the problems was that she didn't give of herself emotionally in the relationship. He wasn't getting what he wanted from her and he didn't have the skills to communicate it, so he retreated into porn. It wasn't her fault or his; it was the couple's fault together. There was a lack of intimacy and connectedness in their relationship, and because of it, she used to shop all the time, and he used to watch porn. They both had their escape mechanisms to not deal with the relationship. When you get to ultimatums about watching porn, it usually means there's a dysfunction in the relationship somewhere else, and the porn is a symptom that you're seeing on the surface. Any time you get to that point, I think a couple needs to talk to a therapist.

Dr. Paula

Unfortunately, there are a lot of women who haven't had an orgasm. However, adding fantasy may be just the thing that allows her to experience that pleasure.

Dr. Reef

Yes, you might be surprised at what can happen when a little imagination is added to the mix. Role-playing, costumes, toys, all sorts of things can liven up sex. Just don't cry out your ex-boyfriend's name during sex; everything else is fair game.

Dr. Paula

Sex should be fun, I agree.

Dr. Reef

TV sex is pretty funny; it lasts like 48 seconds, with really good lighting, and everybody has an orgasm at the exact same time. If only life were that simple.

CHAPTER 5: Problem Solving

As your relationship with another person grows and your lives become more interconnected, issues are bound to come up. The shift from "me" to "we" will make things different — you can count on it. We each tend to think that the way we do things is right and the way the other does things is wrong. If you are a neat freak and subscribe to the "cleanliness is next to godliness" theory, then you might be quite judgmental of his or her messiness. Sometimes the collision of habits can test and sorely try a relationship. As we've said throughout the book, knowing how you deal with conflict will go a long way toward being able to talk with your partner when problems come up. In this chapter, we'll show you how to problem solve, so that conflicts do not consume your relationship.

DEALING WITH CONFLICT

Dr. Paula

Disagreements are a part of every authentic human connection; they offer an opportunity to transform a relationship. Effective conflict-resolution skills are key to a lasting, healthy partnership.

Dr. Reef

To develop those skills, you have to understand what's really triggering the conflict. Couples almost always fight over the exact same things: their unfulfilled desire to be heard, to be respected, to be appreciated, and to be loved. Everyone wants to feel the other is there for them, listening to what they say, and paying attention.

Dr. Paula

When you feel hurt because you don't feel heard or respected, it's not uncommon to try to hurt someone else. It's human nature to try to create in others what we ourselves feel inside. Human beings are animals. We have a very primitive response when we feel under attack. It's called the "fight or flight reaction." When we were dwelling in caves and were about to be attacked by a wild animal, staying still and taking it was not the most effective strategy for perpetuating our species. We are designed to either run away or stay and fight. Even thousands of years later, we have this reaction.

Dr. Reef

People fight in different ways. Some are passive-aggressive, some use anger, some cry, some manipulate.

Studies on the differences in how men and women communicate have shown that women often use an argument as a way to break through barriers and build intimacy in their relationships, while men use communication to find solutions to problems.

Dr. Paula

Yes, there are a few basic ways that people tend to deal with conflict. They:

1) pretend it doesn't exist
2) shut down
3) get defensive
4) try to make peace by glossing over issues
5) deal with it head-on
6) compromise

When women are "fighting," they want to let men know how they feel. They often mix emotional venting with statements of fact. Men, on the other hand, are focused solely on the facts. He may say, *"Just tell me what I need to do."* She may want him to do something differently, but she also wants him to engage in the process of dealing with emotional content. As you can imagine, these fundamental differences can cause misunderstandings, leading him to state, *"She's nuts,"* while she concludes, *"He just doesn't get it."*

Dr. Reef

And these fundamental differences can also reflect power

Dr. Paula: *How Do You Respond to Conflict?*

Each person deals with conflict differently. One person in a relationship may want to talk things out, while the other may hold feelings of anger or resentment inside. What is your particular style? Here are some questions that might help you figure that out:

- Do you deal with conflict calmly and with thoughtful attention to the other person's point of view?

- Do you experience any disagreement as a personal attack on you?

- Are you like a pressure cooker — first you let old stuff build up, and then you explode?

- Are you someone who avoids confrontation at any cost?

- Are you impulsive, saying and doing things you know you shouldn't during an argument, and then regretting it later?

- Do you shut down at the first sign of disagreement or argument?

struggles, particularly in terms of who's making the big decisions, who's compromising, who gets what he or she wants, and who doesn't. For some, it's more important "to be right than to be loved." They'd rather fight to feel right than to have a better relationship.

Dr. Paula

I agree. Many fights can be based on who holds the power. If you've been hurt in your life, you may try to have the upper hand to avoid being hurt again. Unfortunately, if your goal in a relationship is to have more power than your partner, you will likely end up feeling pretty powerless when the other person leaves you. Relationships work best when you see each other as teammates, not rivals.

Dr. Reef

Yes, but there has to be something holding the relationship together. It could be a common upbringing, religion, community, college, humor, etc. The differences between men and women can be good. We don't want to date someone exactly like us (that's what friends are for). We grow more as people when we date people different than ourselves. But if those differences turn into disagreements, it helps to have commonalities as well that will help you resolve your conflicts.

Dr. Paula

The messages you received as a child have a big impact on your current ability to handle conflict. If you grew up in a home where anger was expressed as out-of-control, almost violent behavior, then you might avoid expressing what you really feel until you reach the point of exploding. Then what happens? Your belief that anger = going out of control gets reinforced. If you grew up in a home with a lot of yelling, you might be more comfortable with raising your own voice. If your partner grew up not hearing family members raise their voices, he might be freaked out and scared when you raise your voice. Asking your partner how conflict was handled in his home as a child will help give you (and him) a good idea of what current expectations might be.

Dr. Reef

How we dealt with conflict in our childhood (how our parents resolved issues, how we were treated, how we did or didn't get our needs met) will influence our conflict-resolution skills. When families can discuss disagreements in healthy ways, it's a skill that can be passed down to the kids. Conflict that involves lots of screaming, personal attacks, or violence can also be passed down from generation to generation.

Mad About Money

Dr. Reef

Money is a hot-button topic for most people. Though it can't buy you happiness, it can provide comfort and a sense of security. We all have needs, things we want, whether it has to do with the career we aspire to have, the number of kids we want, the vacation spot we'd like to visit, or even the restaurant we want to go to. Money is required for most things in life. The person who holds the purse strings may end up with more power in the relationship.

Also, money can be used in many ways — to control, to provide for, to help with resources, to exert power and influence, to give in lieu of emotional giving, to pacify or appease someone, to temporarily replace love, to feign interest. You need to be aware of how you're using money in the relationship and how your boyfriend or girlfriend is using it as well. The important thing is to understand why you're using money in all the ways that you do.

Dr. Paula

And, Reef, we know that men and women *think* differently about money. It's one of the top reasons couples divorce. Even if you aren't close to getting engaged, if you are thinking that there might be a future with your current boyfriend or girlfriend, then you have to start talking about money.

Dr. Reef

But, Paula, it's amazing to me how many couples *don't* talk about money. They can talk about their secret fantasies of having wild, reckless sex wearing furry animal suits, but they can't talk about how much money they earn or how much they owe. People would rather speak in public or be held captive in a small foreign country than talk to the person they're dating about their current debt.

Dr. Paula

Timing is key. While on the first date, you wouldn't ask, *"Hey, how much do you make?"* But as a relationship progresses and your lives become more intertwined, it's a completely appropriate question to ask.

Dr. Reef

I agree, Paula. Learning about people's money situation is another way of knowing them; of knowing their past, their secrets, their good — and bad — decisions, their family history, the way their parents dealt with money.

In fact, the way a couple discusses money can be a major predictor of whether their relationship will survive. How each person organizes his or her finances, whether they fight over money, how they prioritize their spending, their savings vs. spending habits, financial secrets . . . these are all potential indicators of the health of the relationship and how the power is structured within the relationship.

Dr. Paula

Do you think it's rude to ask someone how much they make? Did your parents tell you to never talk about money? Well, imagine living with your boyfriend who has had a toothache for a month, and when you ask him why he hasn't had it looked at, he tells you, *"I can't afford to go to the dentist."* If he's unemployed and has no savings, that's one thing. But imagine he makes a six-figure salary. He has an expensive car, the latest of every electronic device that begins with the prefix "i," and yet he can't afford to take care of his health? What does this tell you about his priorities and values? Are they compatible with yours? I'm not saying that you need to dump him, but knowing what he earns gives you an important context in which to understand him and to learn why he does what he does. As relationships get more and more serious, it becomes more and more crucial to talk about finances and money.

Dr. Reef

You could be dating someone and have sex on a regular basis, take vacations together, meet her parents, and know every dream she has in life, but still not know a thing about her financial situation. It could be one of the last aspects she's willing to share freely about herself.

Dr. Paula

There's nothing like money to create friction and conflict. Differences in priorities, values, and the degree of impulsivity vs. the ability to delay gratification become apparent when money is involved. Some of us are very uncomfortable when we don't have a financial safety net, while others seem okay with living paycheck to paycheck. There's the "always save for a rainy day" personality, and the "life's short, have fun!" mentality. Can you imagine the issues that might come up during holidays, birthdays, or planning a trip together? Let's look at what might happen if a saver gets involved with a spender.

Jeff and Annie think of themselves as the poster couple for "opposites attract." He is a T-shirt-and-jeans kind of guy, working in computer technology, and she is a senior manager for a large corporation. He likes action films, and she enjoys anything with a subtitle. They were fine with their differences until they started to live together and decided to open a joint bank account. Jeff is a bit of a tightwad; he's careful to stay on budget so he can occasionally indulge his passion for high-quality electronic equipment. Annie's job requires nice clothes and professional outfits; Jeff considers her a spendthrift when it comes to clothes, and she calls him a miser who only spends money on himself. They both make about the same amount of money, but at the end of the month, when there are still bills to pay, Annie is sometimes out of money. When she recently came home with an expensive outfit, Jeff yelled, "You are so incredibly selfish! I can't believe you're spending our money so recklessly when I'm trying to save for the future."

Dr. Reef

This scenario reflects several key issues about the couple. Annie's job demands that she's smart and well dressed, but if she's short on money at the end of the month, then she needs to decrease her spending and be accountable for paying her share of the bills on time. Jeff could definitely be more understanding of what her job requires, and rather than blaming, help her to understand other priorities now that they are living together.

It's interesting — and it may not be the case here — that research studies show that men and women tend to spend around the same amount of money, but they do it very differently. For women, shopping can be an emotional experience, almost a ritual. For men, the goal is to "get something," not necessarily to enjoy the experience. However, the actual amount of dollars spent tends to even out between them.

Dr. Paula

If you see yourself reflected in this scenario, it's important to learn how to hit your inner "pause" button. Using this skill, instead of leading off with an aggressive reaction, allows you to collect your thoughts and approach your partner with the goal of resolving issues instead of making them worse. You can buy yourself time by breathing deeply, walking away, or perhaps making an appointment with the other person to deal with the issue later. Some couples have a code word they use to stop an interaction before it gets too heated. Some learn to count to ten. Compromise requires a degree of calmness and reason.

As we mentioned in Chapter 1 and earlier in this chapter, your family can influence a lot of your adult habits — and the same is true with how you think about money.

Dr. Reef

Exactly. If your dad was trying to control you with money throughout your childhood, I guarantee you it will affect you in your adult life. You will either spend carelessly *(I never want to be like my parent)*, or you'll be just like him because that's what you know.

As in the scenario above, if you were raised to be "thrifty" and your dating partner was raised to "spend," you're going to need to have a discussion about money pretty soon. Your spending habits will emerge sooner or later anyway, so it's best to have this "crucial conversation" early enough to reach a mutual understanding; you may be able to come to some kind of compromise, or you may find a way to maintain your differences in a healthy way. If you can't reach an agreement that works for both of you, your relationship may encounter serious challenges. . . .

Dr. Paula

Based on my experience working with women in relationships, this is what I have found to be best: you can open a joint bank account, but each of you should also have your own personal account. The purpose of the joint account is to pay shared expenses such as the rent, utilities, and other things that belong to both of you. Each of you should contribute to the account an amount that is proportionate to what you make. Keeping your own bank account helps you feel secure. You don't want to be in a position to stay with someone who isn't right for you just because you can't afford to break up.

Also, having your own account can help avoid some of the questions like, *"Why did you spend so much on that?"* or *"Is that a new pair of boots? You already have ten pairs of black boots that look exactly the same."* If you are earning enough money and can really afford to buy yourself a new pair of boots, you don't want to have to justify your purchases. Sometimes, he may just not understand that, unlike all the other pairs, these boots have a pointed toe and 3-inch heels, and come to the midcalf. Which, of course, is totally different from the ankle boots with the rounded toe and 1.5-inch heel. This is why spending money from your own account is a good idea.

Dr. Reef
I have one pair of black boots and couldn't tell you a single thing about them.

It makes sense to have a joint account for "joint household" bills, and then separate accounts for personal purchases. Once you're married or you've spent a long time together, you could make everything joint, but this is a good way to feel like a couple but still maintain some independence.

Advice from Dr. Reef: *Ten Things Couples Should Agree on When Talking About Money in Their Relationship*

---

1) Who pays for the dates? Is it always the guy? Should the man and woman alternate? Are there special occasions where the other person should pay?

2) Do you have a joint account if you are living together? Do you have separate personal accounts as well?

3) Discuss the relationship that each of your families had with money and how it affected each of you.

4) Figure out how much each of you owes (debt) and your credit ratings, and how that might affect you if you get married.

5) As a couple, do you have any spending limitations? Do you have to check in with each other if you spend more than a certain amount?

6) Should you make some investments? If so, what kind? Do you both want to see a financial adviser to help you with your investments?

7) Do either of you have a gambling or compulsive shopping problem?

8) Are there any major money secrets either of you needs to know about?

9) Who's going to work, and what will each of your contributions be to your shared financial picture as a couple? Will the main financial contributor be more of the decision maker? How do you decide who makes the major decisions and who is assigned to pay the bills?

10) How do you both handle money or extravagant gifts from in-laws and other relatives and friends? If the items you receive are super expensive, or if one set of in-laws gives and the other doesn't, how do you handle that?

Don't forget that one of the reasons people don't come clean about their financial situation is because it may force them to reveal other aspects of their personal life.

"How Could You Forget What Today Is?"

Dr. Paula

Another source of tension between couples that could lead to conflict has to do with expectations — not remembering a birthday or anniversary, for example. Do we put too much significance on whether these occasions are celebrated? Do we assign more importance to a gift or a call than to the actual ongoing nature of the relationship? Let's take a look at Anna and Eric. . . .

 Anna was excited because the one-year anniversary of when she first met and began dating Eric was coming up. It had been a year in which their affection for one another had deepened, and Anna felt he was the first man who truly "got" her, understanding her mercurial moods. She didn't think she needed to drop any clues about the special day, because she was sure he would remember it and want to celebrate it in some way. But when the day came, he didn't call and didn't even send flowers. Anna was devastated and felt angry that their relationship didn't mean as much to Eric as it did to her.

Dr. Reef

Anna is reacting without fully understanding the differences between men and women. Men are single focused. We don't remember symbolic dates because we're not thinking about them. Men think about a specific task with tunnel vision and laser in on it, while women tend to have a more diffuse awareness, with an ability to see and feel more of their environment. Usually, we don't remember the dates until we get some kind of reminder or hint. Either Anna should have mentioned, *"I can't wait for our anniversary next week,"* or left Eric some little note on her planner book that he would be likely to notice. That's when he'd realize, *Oh, yeah, I've got to do something for her.*

Dr. Paula

For Anna, it's not just about remembering the date — it's about what that date represents. Women take the conceptual leap to thinking, *If he remembers our anniversary is April 10, that means he respects me and thinks I'm attractive. If he forgets our anniversary or my birthday, it really means he thinks I'm invisible.*

Dr. Reef

When men do remember, they have every intention of making the woman feel good; it's just that men don't usually attach as much of an emotional response to a symbolic gesture or date. This is why men don't quite "get" why it's so important to women, and they have to cross the perceptual line of understanding to appreciate how much it means to her.

Dr. Paula

So, what you're saying is that in the scenario, Anna is ascribing much more meaning to the occasion than she needs to. She's making it about the flowers, but it's really not about that. She may think Eric doesn't care about her, but that's not the case.

Dr. Reef

I don't think Anna should take it so personally if Eric forgets their one-year anniversary. If he doesn't treat her well *and* he doesn't remember her special dates, that's a different story. But if he's a good guy who treats her well, but he doesn't remember certain details, then I say she should let it go. If an anniversary or birthday is that important to her, I think she should remind him it's coming up. She should rent a billboard if she has to.

Dr. Paula

It comes back to the fundamental differences between men and women.

Dr. Reef

Yes, and not just emotional differences, but biological as well. A woman's hippocampus and the way she processes memories and emotional responses is different from a man's. Because of that, women are more clued in to remembering certain things that they attach emotional value to.

Each couple has a unique way of communicating. The key is for them to come up with a system that works for *both* of them. This is the best way to solve a problem — to discuss it. They each need to let the other know how they feel — what's important to them and why.

IT'S THE LITTLE THINGS . . .

Dr. Reef

Many couples fight over trivial things, like who gets to pick the restaurant for dinner or why someone left dirty laundry on the floor. It's called "the superficial issue." The deeper issue is almost always: *I don't feel loved, respected, or appreciated.* It's harder to verbalize those feelings, so most couples fight about something that doesn't strike such a personal chord. An argument over who makes the dinner plans becomes a stand-in for much larger issues of not feeling appreciated or respected. Developing good conflict-resolution skills is a process of learning how to communicate emotionally. When you invest time and effort in doing this, you greatly improve your chances of staying together.

Dr. Paula

Sometimes the argument is about the dishes in the sink, and sometimes it's about who spent more money on a Valentine's gift, but more often than not, the arguments are about less obvious matters.

We redirect our anger, venting at a "safer" target. This concept, known as "displacement," is basically a defense mechanism that we use without even being aware that we are doing it. Let's look at the scenario of Terri and Dan:

 Terri had a bad day at work because her boss yelled at her for making a mistake that cost the company time and money. She knew she couldn't yell back if she expected to keep her job. So what did she do with her feelings of anger and frustration? When she came home and saw her boyfriend Dan's shoes and socks scattered on the floor, she began to yell at him, "I'm tired of you leaving your crap all over the place!"

Dr. Paula

She displaced her anger and vented at Dan — but at the

expense of her relationship with him. What could she have done differently? When she comes home from her bad day at work, Terri could share with Dan what happened, talking openly about how it felt to make that mistake and be yelled at by her boss.

Which approach do you think would be better for your relationship, and your own mental health? Any time you have a reaction that seems seriously disproportionate to the problem, ask yourself what's really going on. What are you so angry about? I believe this is one of the most important skills to develop and use when conflict erupts.

Dr. Reef

A good relationship will make each person strive to be better. And constant yelling or nagging is a really quick way to kill a relationship. A person can only take so much negativity. The "negative" person in the relationship either needs to become more supportive or go to therapy to work out his or her own personal issues.

Your Cheat Sheet on . . . Cheating

 Kristie and Paul have been dating for five months, and though they've encountered the occasional "bump in the road" (an argument about getting together more often, or whether or not to rent a place for the summer), it hasn't been anything they haven't been able to resolve. In general, they've been happy with each other and considerate of one another's needs. Then, Kristie begins to notice Paul becoming more distant and irritable. Finally, one night he confesses to her that he's "slipped" and cheated

on her while she was on a work-related trip the week before. When she hears this, she becomes furious and doesn't know how to deal with her intense feelings of jealousy. It's the first time this has happened, but she doesn't know if she can forgive him. What can she do?

Dr. Reef

Kristie's response is natural. Generally, the first response someone has when they find out they've been cheated on is to get really pissed off. When you get angry, the other person gets defensive and won't reveal as much information, but you need more information to make a conscious decision about moving forward. Instead of getting upset right way, it's a good idea to take some time to sort through the facts to find out what really happened.

Dr. Paula

Because this is the first time this has happened and Paul has told Kristie fairly soon, that's a much better scenario than if she finds out some other way or if she discovers that he's "slipped" multiple times. Sometimes, when people are moving on to the next level of the relationship, they get a little freaked out and they cheat. They can't deal with the increasing emotional intimacy.

Dr. Reef

I agree — the subtext here is important. *Why* is Paul cheating? If it was a drunk, random encounter, was he trying to self-sabotage? Did he start to fear the intimacy of the relationship? Or was there some other ulterior motive going on? If he didn't tell Kristie about the encounter right way, she should ask, why not? Since he *does* confess immediately, what made him want to tell her? Kristie needs to gather a lot of data to make a good decision about what to do.

Dr. Paula

Another thing to take into account is whom he's cheating with. If it's with one of his exes, are there still unresolved feelings? If he's cheated once with someone that he just randomly hooked up with, that's something she can move through more easily than if it was with an ex.

But either way, issues of trust are involved, and he has to be accountable and be willing to work at building that trust back. He's got to let Kristie know where he is at all times. This example is about a man cheating, but it just as well could be about a woman who slips. If you're the one who's been cheated on, you need to see that he's willing to prove to you — by his actions — that he's going to be faithful from now on. He has to be willing to be fully transparent to earn your trust back. If he can't agree to that, I think all bets are off.

Dr. Reef

A big problem here is if Kristie becomes overrun with jealousy, it could be really difficult to move on in the relationship.

Dr. Paula

Absolutely. If she decides she's going to stay with Paul and move forward, even though he's cheated on her, then she needs to let go of her feelings of anger and resentment. If she forgives him, it doesn't justify what he did. It doesn't mean she has to forget it. And it doesn't mean she's naïve or a doormat. But it's important for her to let go of the negative charge of the whole transgression, because she can't stay with the guy *and* be pissed at him all the time and try to get revenge or make him pay for what he did. That's a sure way for the relationship not to work.

Dr. Reef

It requires a lot of strength for her to let go of those negative emotions and move on.

Dr. Paula

If she's not willing to do this, then she's setting herself up to be absolutely miserable.

Dr. Reef

Yes, and she shouldn't feel that because Paul cheated on her, she has a free pass to cheat on him, too. That's weak thinking.

Dr. Paula

In order to problem solve and get the relationship back on track, she's got to be firm. If he cheated with his ex, there needs to be 100 percent agreement that he will cut off all contact with her. He has to show that he's willing to repair the relationship. If he's not willing to let go of her, then he's not putting a very high value on his relationship with Kristie.

Dr. Reef

I would recommend couples therapy. I did relationship therapy with one couple where he had cheated with his ex, and the girlfriend wanted him to stop seeing the other woman totally. He said that he had known his ex for eight years, and they were still friends, and it was just a brief slipup. He and his current girlfriend reached a compromise: he couldn't have any contact with his ex for six months, and after that, if there was any contact, it had to be minimal, in public, and always in the presence of his current girlfriend.

Dr. Reef: *Questions to Ask Your Partner When He or She Has Cheated*

- Who is the person you cheated with? (Is it a friend? Someone from your workplace?)

- Are you in love with this person?

- Was this spontaneous or predetermined?

- Were you drunk, high, or altered in any way?

- How many times has this happened? For how long?

- Why do you think it happened?

- What events in our relationship could have contributed to this happening?

- Have you ever done this before in our relationship or other relationships?

- Would you be willing to talk to a professional about this?

- What exactly happened to lead to the cheating?

CONTROL ISSUES

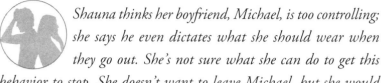 *Shauna thinks her boyfriend, Michael, is too controlling; she says he even dictates what she should wear when they go out. She's not sure what she can do to get this behavior to stop. She doesn't want to leave Michael, but she would like to keep the relationship moving forward on more equal footing. Shauna wonders, What can I do to solve this problem?*

Dr. Paula

You go first, Reef. I'm trying to be less controlling!

Dr. Reef

You do it well.

Dr. Paula

What, talk about control in relationships or be controlling?

Dr. Reef

I'm keeping it general. I actually think that control is one of those deep psychological issues that is difficult for a couple to resolve.

If Shauna thinks her boyfriend is controlling, it usually means: a) he really *is* too controlling, or b) she's had some issues in her childhood that are causing her to see Michael as being too controlling as he gets more emotionally intimate with her. His letting her know which outfit she looks good in may actually be emotionally controlling behavior, but it may also be him just complimenting her on outfits; with her emotional history, that gets perceived as being controlling. This has to be worked through by the two of them together or with a therapist.

Dr. Paula

There's a wide range of what we consider to be controlling behavior. As Reef said, part of this is dictated by your childhood and what your perceptions are. Some guys think that if their girlfriend asks them to call her once a day, she's being controlling. A more extreme example is a guy who tells his girlfriend what she can and can't eat because he won't allow her to gain a pound.

If you're with someone that you perceive to be controlling, there are things you can do to retrain him or her. For example, let's say your boyfriend texts you five times a day because he wants to check in, and he gets mad if you don't text him back. If you always respond to every single text of his, you're supporting his behavior. You're encouraging it. Instead, you could say to him, *"Listen, I know you have a need to text me five times a day, but I'm not going to text you back every time. I'll text you back once."* If the relationship is otherwise stable, hopefully he'll say, *"Okay, fine."* You respond once to his texts, and though he may be irritated you're not responding more frequently, he's willing to accept your boundaries. In this scenario, I don't think you need to dump the relationship.

Sometimes, especially early in the relationship, a woman may be insecure, and so some of her behavior may be about her need to be reassured that her boyfriend is thinking about her. She may call ten times a day, but it's just to allay her own anxieties. He can say to her, *"Listen, I care about you. I'm sorry I don't pick up my phone when I'm at work during the day. If that's what you need from me, then this isn't going to work out — but it's not that I don't care about you.*" If he thinks about why she's doing what she's doing, he may be able to give her the reassurance she needs — and help her change her behavior.

Dr. Reef

There are different types of controlling. When someone is insecure and controlling, it's more about the "controller" needing to be soothed. Then there's "pathological controlling." That's entirely different; that's when someone controls another person for his or her own benefit, so that the other person can't be who they are.

Dr. Paula

Right. If he doesn't want you going out with your girlfriends, if she doesn't want you watching your favorite sports team, that's being overly controlling — the message they're sending is that it's not okay to be who you are. When someone tries to stop you from being happy or keeps you from realizing your goals or dreams, that's a serious problem. We see this sometimes in parent/child dynamics, where the adult is controlling the child's world and trying to keep him or her dependent. What ultimately happens, of course, is that the young person grows up and leaves. If you have a boyfriend or girlfriend who has such serious, controlling behavior, you may have no other option but to get out.

A Tip from Dr. Reef: *What to Say When Your Boyfriend or Girlfriend Begins to Get Too Controlling*
"I'm a person with my own identity, background, and life. I'm trying to share my life with you, but if you continue to act so controlling with me, you're going to suffocate me emotionally and cause me to want to leave this relationship. You can't own me."

INVASION OF PRIVACY

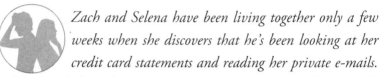 *Zach and Selena have been living together only a few weeks when she discovers that he's been looking at her credit card statements and reading her private e-mails. When she asks him about it, he apologizes profusely and admits that he was doing it to get to know her better. Selena feels "creeped out" by this invasion of privacy and isn't sure how to stop it from happening again.*

Dr. Paula

Zach may be paranoid and insecure, but it's still a major violation of Selena's privacy. When two people move in together, it's important to establish boundaries from the get-go. Having a conversation about this early on forces people to figure out what they're comfortable with. What's normal for you? If you grew up with six siblings, you are probably not used to much privacy. If you were an only child and grew up in a formal home where nobody went into Dad's study, you're probably going to feel differently. A lot of times, people haven't spent any time evaluating their own comfort level on these issues.

Some people don't care if their boyfriend or girlfriend has all their passwords and opens their mail. Others have a rigid sense of privacy and would be appalled to have anybody else reading their e-mails or letters. No matter what your background is, it's a pretty serious thing if someone suspects that you're cheating and needs to snoop on you to find out what you're up to. Is it an issue that you can't overcome? Not necessarily. But it is a tough problem.

Dr. Reef

If you go through someone else's stuff — whether you feel you have "probable cause" or you're just overly curious — it's not going to be a one-time thing. Once Zach started, he won't be able to stop. The first time he did it, he may feel a little guilty, but after he gets over it, he'll find it easier to do a second time . . . because he's already done it. It's a definite problem that he can only relieve by understanding *why* he's doing it.

Dr. Paula

I think people need to have a "crucial conversation" about privacy up front, just to set the ground rules.

Dr. Reef

If a woman said to me, *"Let's talk about e-mails and what I can and can't go through. How should we deal with passwords? Is it okay if I go through your mail?"* I'd think she was psycho. Most guys would. You have to be really careful about how you bring this topic up, because it could backfire — big time. It would be better to start the conversation by saying, *"Some people accidentally leave their e-mail or Facebook accounts open.*

What should we do if that happens and we're tempted to read it?" If you're not living together, you should talk in generalities about the concept rather than personalizing it. This is what I call the "prevention script," where you use hypotheticals to get your point across.

Then, there's the "intervention script," which happens after you've caught somebody going through your things.

Dr. Paula

The intervention script should be very direct. For example: *"When I saw you going through my mail, it made me feel really angry and confused about why you would do that. Help me understand what was going on."* You've got to wait until you're in a calm frame of mind, as Reef said earlier. If you display anger, the other person is going to shut down. Gather your thoughts together. Remember, the formula to use is, *"When you do (x) . . . I feel (y)."* You're talking about how his action made you feel rather than just accusing. *"When you look at messages on my iPhone while I'm in the shower, I feel like my privacy's been violated. If you have questions for me, feel free to ask me, instead of taking it into your own hands to snoop through my things."*

Dr. Reef

There are different types of snooping. There's "crisis" snooping, which occurs when you say to yourself, *I think she's cheating on me, and I have to find out for sure.*

Dr. Paula

You believe you have probable cause.

Dr. Reef

Yes. Then, there's what I call "maintenance" snooping: you don't have any reason, you don't suspect her of anything, you just want to know more about her.

Dr. Paula

Of course, sometimes in the process of maintenance snooping, you may actually find evidence that your boyfriend is cheating on you. When you bring it up, he may say, *"I can't believe you went through my stuff. You violated my rights!"* Which is his diversionary tactic to deflect attention from his own actions.

Dr. Reef

Also, Paula, I'm sure you've seen this in couples therapy, too — the one who's doing the snooping and actively going after the other person for cheating usually turns out to have a history of cheating in the past.

Dr. Paula

That's right. We tend to project onto other people what we know to be true about ourselves. If I'm someone who's been unfaithful, I'm much more likely to accuse my boyfriend of being unfaithful.

Of course, as we've said, people snoop for all kinds of reasons. Some are incredibly curious, and others are just incredibly insecure.

Dr. Reef

No matter what the reason is, I think snooping is potentially the death of the relationship. A big part of being in a relationship is that each person has to respect the separate identity of the other. Otherwise, you have an unhealthy or codependent relationship. If you're someone who snoops, you're saying, *It makes me feel insecure not to be completely part of the other person's world.* Ultimately, the message is: *I don't want the other person to have a separate identity,* and that's very unhealthy.

Dr. Paula

If you have the urge to snoop, you need to tell your boyfriend or girlfriend. In order to stop this behavior, you're going to have to go through snooping withdrawl.

Dr. Reef

Your partner can actually help you. He or she can provide you with more information verbally. For example, your partner can say, *"You want to know something about me? Let me tell you something about myself you don't know. . . ."*

Dr. Paula

What you're doing is getting to the heart of the issue, which may not be the snooping but your sense of insecurity and wanting to be part of your partner's world. Let's say a woman has a boyfriend who's very rigid about his privacy, because of the way he was raised or simply because of his personality. She may start projecting onto him because she doesn't have enough to go on. He's like a walking Rorschach test for her. In order to stop the snooping, it's important to understand the *why* behind it. That's the whole premise of our book. In this case, by having a clearer sense of *why* she's snooping, she can do something about it so it doesn't continue. As Reef said, if the guy is willing to share more details about his life, it may be a way to help her get over her need to snoop. By doing that, they may actually be saving their relationship.

STRATEGIES FOR RESOLVING CONFLICT

Dr. Paula

In this section, we're going to look at practical and successful strategies for resolving conflict. One of the most important tools to use is also the most basic: one-to-one communication.

Dr. Reef

That's right. What we're talking about here is a healthy discussion where each person can participate in "active listening" (actually listening to the other person without just thinking defensively about one's own self) and can "cross the perceptual line" (putting oneself in the other person's position). The ability to do both is crucial to the problem-solving process. Each person in a relationship needs to be heard and respected. That's the key.

The couples who have the healthiest relationships tend to have the strongest conflict-resolution skills. The best way to work out a problem is to:

1) fight with mutual respect
2) show appreciation for the other person's point of view
3) be able to relate to his or her feelings

If you personalize a conflict or attack the other person's core identity — family, religion, psychological history, etc. — you end up causing damage that may be difficult to repair. Keep the fight focused on the subject at hand. And remember, conflict resolution is about compromise; two people meeting halfway to solve a problem. A lot of relationship conflict resolution is about picking your battles and knowing when to really stand up for yourself and when to let the other person have what they need.

Dr. Paula

Also, just keep in mind why you are compromising. Sometimes you have to ask yourself, *Do I want to be right or do I want to be happy?* A friend recently shared with me an interesting approach to compromise. When he and his wife disagree about something important, they take a step back and ask, *"Who feels more strongly about this?"* The key to this is that they are always able to agree on who feels more strongly about the issue. And that's how their arguments get resolved.

Dr. Reef

Healthy communication and respect will always improve a relationship and help to avoid major conflict. But every relationship has conflict. Conflict is natural in a relationship. It's how you solve the conflict that's crucial to the survival of the relationship.

Dr. Paula

You don't just brush your teeth when they hurt, right? Just like your teeth, relationships require daily maintenance. You have to brush in order to prevent plaque and tartar from building up. You have to talk and listen in order to help prevent the buildup of resentment.

Build up a "positive relationship bank account." If most of your interactions are good, then you can weather some difficult times. Research shows that for every negative interaction you need about nine positive interactions to counteract it. Make sure to have fun together.

Dr. Reef

Men need to practice listening more to their partner. Even if they don't agree with her, they can respect her opinion and appreciate her.

Dr. Paula

Women can practice "hitting the pause button" (as described earlier) when things are getting too emotional. They need to discuss the rules for fighting fair (see pages 187–188) with their partner and agree to use them as much as possible. Sometimes just knowing you can handle conflict can help you avoid it.

A Tip from Dr. Paula

A valuable strategy is the art of the "soft start." Despite what you may hear, there's no need to share every thought and feeling. Like the raw ingredients in a cupcake — flour, baking soda, and salt — on their own they are not so tasty, but once they've been mixed and baked they are ready to be enjoyed. The same can be true for feelings and thoughts. Give yourself some time before launching into whatever is bothering you. A woman has the ability to "soft start" a conversation, to ease into an issue versus aggressively laying it on.

PROBLEM SOLVING: HOW TO FIGHT FAIR

Dr. Paula

A friend of mine recently said, *"In an argument, you can choose to throw water or fuel on the fire . . . and in an argument, fireworks are overrated."* So true! Are you going to be an arsonist or a firefighter? Let's look at the couple in the scenario below to see if they're throwing water or fuel on their fire. . . .

 It started at 6:15 a.m. as Lara was blow-drying her hair. Though Tyler was still asleep, she wasn't going to let that stop her from getting herself ready for work.

"What's with all the friggin' noise?" Tyler shouted, his voice hoarse and groggy.

"I'm getting ready for work. Some of us have jobs and responsibilities, you know," Lara snapped back. *"You might be able to sleep away the entire day, but I can't."*

"Hey," Tyler said, sitting up in bed, *"I can't help it if I can't find a job."*

"Well, it would help if you would start looking," Lara said, turning the switch on the blow-dryer to high so it was even louder.

"Who died and made you my mother?" Tyler yelled.

"I am not your mother," she hollered over the noise of the blow-dryer. *"I'm your girlfriend, and I'm tired of picking up after you as if you were a child. I'm tired of you always forgetting to do the grocery shopping when I've asked you a million times. You always think about yourself. You never think about me!"*

"That's not true," said Tyler, "I went grocery shopping two weeks ago!"

Dr. Paula

Lara and Tyler were producing some fireworks that weren't pretty. What could they have done differently to shift from unfair to fair fighting? They could follow these three strategies:

1) Stay calm. Ty and Laura get worked up and accelerate from 0 to 120. (Ty immediately shouts, *"What's with all the friggin' noise?"* and Lara snaps back, *"Some of us have jobs and responsibilities, you know. You might be able to sleep away the entire day, but I can't."*) The calmer that Ty is, the more likely it is that Lara will respond similarly. The calmer that Lara is, the more likely it is that Tyler will actually hear what she's saying. When she's yelling and screaming at him, he's going to go on the defensive or shut down. That's a natural human tendency.

2) Avoid the kitchen sink. Women are often guilty of throwing everything into the fight, instead of just arguing the issue at hand. In this case, Lara brings up a bunch of other stuff about Tyler that's been bothering her (*". . . I'm tired of picking up after you as if you were a child. I'm tired of you always forgetting to do the grocery shopping when I've asked you a million times. You always think about yourself. You never think about me!"*)

3) Never use "never" and "always." When you use absolute terms, you can actually diminish your position. The listener will immediately find examples to refute what

you're saying instead of listening to you. In the scenario above, the minute Lara drags grocery shopping into the fight, Tyler focuses only on that and comes up with proof that he doesn't always forget to shop. And there goes Lara's whole message. A better approach for Lara to take would be to concentrate on what's really bothering her, and to use the *"When I see____, I feel _____"* formula for expressing her emotions. Let's see how Tyler and Lara can use these techniques to talk so they really hear one another:

The next morning, Lara wakes up at her usual time of 6:00 a.m. But before jumping into the shower, she gently strokes Tyler's face. *"Ty,"* she says softly, as he sleeps soundly beside her. *"I have to get up now. I'm giving you fair warning before I start blow-drying my hair."*

"Okay, I'll get up," says Tyler sleepily. *"I know I shouldn't sleep in every morning."*

"Ty," replies Lara, *"it's just that when I see you sleeping in while I have to go to work, I feel frustrated. If we were both working, we could afford a nicer place. Can we come up with a plan so that each of us is pulling our own weight?"*

"Okay," Tyler says, sitting up. *"I hear you. Maybe I can go grocery shopping later so you don't have to worry about that."*

"Thanks," says Lara. *"I really appreciate it when you step up to the plate."*

Rules from the Ring

Before you enter the ring and get into a fighting match, here are some questions you may want to answer:

- What is really bothering me?
- Am I going to just vent or is there some outcome I'd like from this discussion?
- Do I feel like I have to win or do I see us as being on the same team?

Dr. Paula

In the next scenario, we'll look at another couple who creates more problems for themselves by the way they fight:

 Stacey and Ethan were having a tense dinner at home. They were supposed to be going out, but Ethan had forgotten that Stacey had made plans for them to go to a party at their friends' house. When he came home, he said he needed to be working on his company's annual report after dinner.

"You don't have to give me the silent treatment," said Ethan.

Stacey just stared stonily at him and took another bite of the sushi leftover from the night before. "What do you expect? I had a terrible day, and it doesn't seem like the night's going to be much better."

"What does that mean?" asked Ethan.

"You know exactly what that means," Stacey shot back. "We had a party to go to tonight at Andy and Nancy's!"

"I didn't remember, okay?" said Ethan. "I have to work on the company report."

"You never listen to me," Stacey seethed. "All you care about is your work."

"Look who's talking," Ethan sneered. "You're so addicted to your work, you should be in rehab."

"That's what I mean," Stacey replied. "You give me a hard time without even thinking about how this is all your fault."

Ethan paused and then said, "I'm sorry, my bad."

Stacey got up from the table and said, "It's too late for sorrys now."

Dr. Paula

Stacey and Ethan are taking a bad situation and making it worse. But there are strategies they can use to improve their communication so that they're fighting fairly:

1) Use words to express feelings. This is good advice for toddlers and grown-ups. It sounds like a simple thing, but we all know how hard it can be to be rational and to choose our words carefully when we're feeling overwhelmed, angry, or hurt. Stacey and Ethan aren't expressing their feelings — they're just lashing out at each other.

2) Specific is better than vague. When Stacey says, *"You never listen to me,"* that's a hard thing for Ethan to try to address. Stacey needs to be crystal clear, saying: *"Remember last Wednesday, when I told you about tonight's party at Andy and Nancy's while we were watching TV, and you said that you were available to go? When you say you don't remember, it makes me feel like you aren't listening to me."*

3) Don't hit below the belt. When Ethan says, *"You're so addicted to your work, you should be in rehab,"* that's a low blow. We each know what our partner's vulnerabilities might be. While it might be tempting to go in for the kill during an argument, don't. You can't take words back, and when you hit below the belt you erode trust.

4) Talk about specific actions, not sweeping personality traits. Instead of saying, "All you care about is your work," Stacey can talk about how Ethan didn't make an effort to include the party in his schedule.

5) Allow for the U-turn. If, during an argument, your partner apologizes or tries to lighten the mood, that's a step in the right direction. However, in this scenario, when Ethan does apologize, Stacey is dismissive. Couples in good relationships are skilled at responding to a positive change in direction during conflict. It's tempting when we are upset to dig in our heels, but if you want a mature relationship, then you need to act like an adult — not a kid.

Dr. Reef

The common problematic theme here is someone getting upset and taking a specific conflict situation and generalizing it by calling the other person names or calling out their overall character or blaming them for their actions instead of saying how it makes the individual feel.

Dr. Paula

Let's see how Stacey and Ethan can engage in the techniques of fighting fair:

"I really was looking forward to the party tonight at Andy and

Nancy's," says Stacey.

"Stacey, it just slipped my mind that the party was tonight," says Ethan.

Stacey replies, *"Remember last Wednesday, when I told you about tonight's party at Andy and Nancy's while we were watching TV, and you said that you were available to go? When you say you don't remember, it makes me feel like you aren't listening to me."*

"I just have a lot on my mind," says Ethan.

"I know," Stacey responds, *"but it would help if you could make more of an effort to include our personal plans in your schedule."*

"I'm sorry, my bad," says Ethan.

"Thanks," says Stacey, *"I appreciate your saying that."*

 Jillian feels like her boyfriend, Cooper, doesn't really listen to her when she tells him how she feels. "I can see that glazed look in his eyes, like he's trying to stay awake, and that's not very reassuring or supportive if I'm telling him about a tough day at work or problems I'm having with my mom. He says he cares about me, but I'm not sure what I can do to get him to tune into what I'm saying and be responsive."

Dr. Reef

Jillian will want to consider why Cooper isn't listening to her. Some reasons could be:

1) He's purposely not listening to her because he doesn't

agree with her and doesn't want to start a conflict.

2) He's purposely not listening because he doesn't respect her.

3) He's got something else going on at that moment and is focused on that.

4) He's a self-absorbed narcissist who isn't capable of listening to her.

Cooper tells Jillian he wants to go to a baseball game, but she thought they were going to do something on the weekend. Let's examine two approaches. . . .

What not to say:

Cooper: *I want to go to the game with the guys.*

Jillian: *Go ahead, I don't care.* (But she really does care.)

Dr. Reef

This is a common conflict. Cooper says he wants to go. Jillian doesn't say how she really feels. She may hold her emotions (anger, resentment, etc.) inside and then eventually blow up later. He may come home after the game and she will be upset or give him the cold shoulder. This conflict could have been avoided using effective communication up front.

Here's a better approach:

Cooper: *I'd really like to go to the game on Saturday with the guys — it's important to me. Our whole group hasn't seen each other in a while, and this will be a good chance to catch up.*

Jillian: *I thought we planned on going to the museum this weekend. Can't you see them another time?*

Cooper: *Can we go on Sunday instead?*

They need to talk about this to work out their feelings. Then he should either go or not go — but they should both be in agreement.

Let's look at another scenario. Jillian is almost out the front door when she speaks to Cooper, who is resting on the couch.

What not to say:

Jillian: *I'm going to buy new living-room furniture.*

Cooper: *You're always making these financial decisions. Why can't I make any decisions?*

Jillian: *I make the money, that's why.*

Dr. Reef

This is a tougher conflict to solve. If one person makes the money and the other person doesn't feel included when financial decisions are being made, then the couple has to make adjustments.

Here's a better approach:

Jillian: *I've been reviewing our finances, and I think we're in a good place where we can finally get some new furniture.*

Cooper: *Great. When do you want to go shopping?*

Dr. Reef

They could divide up their responsibilities and make sure they both have a voice in the relationship. Since Jillian makes more money, she may have more to say regarding some things, but Cooper could have more say with the children, vacations, family, etc. It's important to recognize that money should not equal supreme power in a relationship because the other person will eventually become resentful.

John tells Victoria that he's invited the guys over to watch a game. The truth is, his buddies are there every Monday night. Victoria likes to go to bed early, John's a night owl. She has a corporate job with a strict schedule, he works from home and feels left out of the social scene. She's not happy with the late-night hours, he's the happiest he's been in months. When they speak to one another, there are things that are not being said. Which means there is an opportunity for compromise.

Dr. Paula
Here's what not to say:

John: *I invited the guys to come over tonight for* Monday Night Football.

Victoria: *I hope it will be over early. Do you think you could tell them to keep it down a little?*

John: *Don't worry, we're not loud.*

Here's what to say:

John: *I'm thinking about asking the guys to come over for the football game, and if it works, it would be a weekly thing — what do you think about that?*

Victoria: *That sounds like fun! My only concern is that I get up early and need a good sleep. But let's give it a try, and if it doesn't work out, maybe you can alternate weeks with the guys.*

Dr. Paula
Now let's look at the same first scenario again, as it progresses from bad to worse:

Here's what not to say:

John: *I invited the guys to come over tonight for* Monday Night Football.

195

Victoria: *I hope it will be over early. Do you think you could tell them to keep it down a little?*

John: *Don't worry, we're not loud.*

Victoria: (with a loud sigh) *Yes, you are. I can barely get to sleep on Monday nights because of your friends.*

John: *I don't have to take being insulted by you!*

Victoria: *Why are you being so hostile? I think you should apologize.*

John: *Why should I?*

Victoria: *You get me so angry. . . .*

Dr. Paula

Now let's look at the aftermath of this disagreement and see how John can take the opportunity to make things better by apologizing:

John: *I'm sorry for speaking to you like that. I didn't mean to lose my cool.*

Victoria: *I appreciate your saying that. I really don't want us to be angry at each other.*

John: *I promise, next time I have the guys over, I'll tell them to keep their voices down.*

Dr. Paula

In the end, the ability to make an apology is an important part of a healthy relationship. When women think they've messed up, they apologize. Generally, men seem to think that apologies are a sign of weakness, and there's concern that it will cause them to lose the respect of others. In the workplace, women are often viewed as being weak if they are too apologetic; in the same situation, men are viewed as arrogant if they don't take ownership of situations where they made a mistake. Women feel they have everything to gain (connections, relationships) with an apology, while men feel they have lots to lose (respect, power, prestige).

Dr. Reef

A man's ego can get in the way of apologizing. Because men have historically been programmed to be the problem solvers, it's hard for them to admit they're wrong or to recognize their emotional limitations. Men also simply don't agree sometimes when a woman gets upset. They don't feel the need to apologize if they don't think the situation is something to be upset about. It's hard to apologize when you don't agree. The apology then becomes about wanting the other person to feel better rather than agreeing with that person.

Dr. Paula

Acknowledging a mistake and making a commitment to try to improve can go a very long way. However, "sorrys" only go so far if future behavior doesn't change.

Dr. Reef

It's important to accept other people for who they are — including their limitations. Nobody is going to be perfect. When you say, *"I'm sorry,"* you're saying to the other person, *"I know I didn't handle that as well as I could and I respect you and love you, so I'd like to apologize for my actions."*

A Tip from Dr. Paula
Six Steps to Making an Effective Apology

1) Describe what you did, and be specific. Your partner needs to know that you truly understand what you did.

2) Acknowledge and express that you recognize the damage and pain you caused.

3) Take responsibility for your part and don't blame the other person.

4) Tell your partner what you would do if you had a chance for a do over. What amends can you offer?

5) Ask for forgiveness.

6) Share your plan for what you will do in the future to prevent this from happening again.

CHAPTER 6: Making a Commitment

At different times in a relationship, we are faced with certain decisions. At first, the question is, "Do I want to go out with this person?" but as time goes on you may ask yourself, "Do I want to see this person exclusively?" Eventually, the questions may take on even greater significance and are no longer questions you ask yourself — they are questions you ask each other: "Should we move in together?" "Does it feel like the right time to get engaged?" "Do we both want to commit, or should we move on?"

Figuring out where you are in a relationship and where you want to be takes reflection and courage. Asking yourself questions (reflection) and then answering them honestly (courage) will help you decide whether to ask these questions of the person you've been dating. Together, you'll discover whether to take your relationship on that quantum leap to the next step.

A Work in Progress

Dr. Paula

Commitment means different things to different people. Don't assume that you share the same definition. Before making a decision, take time to figure out where you are at before worrying about where they might be. Take time to reflect and have the courage to ask the hard questions of yourself and of them.

Dr. Reef

Commitment means more than just sleeping with one person and not dating other people. It also means being open and receptive to an emotional connection with one person and growing and developing as an individual with that person. It can be a wonderful thing, but it shouldn't be taken lightly. Ask yourself, *Why do I want a commitment with this specific person?* And ask yourself if you're ready to take this challenge. With the right person, it'll be worth it.

Dr. Paula

Relationships are a lot like exercising. If you decide one day, *I am going to start running,* what is going to happen? How long will a one-time decision last? To honor a commitment to a healthier life, each day you have to choose to get up, put your sneakers on, and go to the gym. Making a commitment to yourself and to another person is not a one-time event. It's an ongoing process. That's what choosing one person exclusively is all about.

Dr. Reef
Exclusivity: one simple word that can elicit pure joy or total terror. It's a commitment-phobic person's nightmare.

The decision to move forward to an exclusive relationship should start by considering a few questions:

- What am I looking for?
- Am I emotionally ready?
- Am I over my ex?
- Have I recovered from the hurt of past relationships?
- Have I acknowledged the part I played in unsuccessful relationships?
- Am I happy on my own?
- Is he or she "the one"? What qualities does "the one" have?
- Have I learned how to speak up for myself?
- Do I love the person I am?
- Do I understand that I may have to make compromises?
- How does this person make me feel about myself?

Life (and relationships) is a work in progress. Some people are ready for relationships, while others need to spend more time on themselves. If you are ready for it, a committed relationship can be a wonderful thing. It means you're ready and willing to be more emotionally intimate with another person. It'll test your interpersonal skills and teach you about yourself. However, making a commitment with someone because you're broke, or because you're lonely and want a roommate, usually doesn't lead to good things.

Dr. Paula

Right. One of the motivators in taking things to a more serious level is when a couple says, let's be exclusive. That designates a relationship as more than just casual dating.

Ask yourself a simple, straightforward question: *Do I feel like this person can help me grow or not?* You're going to have friction, fights, issues. One of the key areas to consider when moving to the next step is how do you, as a couple, resolve conflict? It doesn't necessarily matter what your specific issues are — some other questions to think about:

- Have I learned the difference between "me" and "we"?
- As a couple, do we satisfactorily handle the rough spots?
- Do we fight fair?
- When I ask for what I want and he can't give it to me, then what? Is that a reason to break up?

Dr. Reef

When he starts thinking, *Wow, I could really hang out with her for the long term, I miss her when we're apart,* that's a good sign he's ready to take the relationship to the next step, and that may be exclusivity. But, as we discussed in Chapter 3, when you meet someone new — and this goes for men and women — and you sense a connection, the biological and novelty part of the encounter (neurochemical) may be tricking you into thinking the relationship is more solid than it really is. There's a rush in meeting and connecting with someone new who you find attractive and interesting.

Not to put a damper on the romantic aspect of this, but that neurochemical rush is one of the reasons falling in love is considered the most wonderful feeling in the world. Over time, it fades and is usually replaced with something else; there still might be a rush here and there, but in order for the relationship to be sustained, the brain's activity will need to shift to promoting an emotional connection. That individual and the relationship should help you grow emotionally as a person.

To Be or Not to Be . . . Monogamous

Dr. Reef

There was a study done recently at Oregon State University that appeared in the *Journal of Sex Research*. Researchers were looking at 434 heterosexual married and non-married American couples, between the ages of 18 and 25, to get their thoughts on the importance of monogamy in a relationship. What they found was that in 40 percent of the couples, one partner said they would be monogamous, while the other partner would not commit to monogamy. The *Journal of Sex Research* article about the study notes that people's definitions of monogamy are different, and not everyone thinks that monogamy is necessary to being in a relationship.

Does that mean that relationships where people aren't on the same page about monogamy are problematic? The authors of the article mention that in terms of relationships, the one predictor for sustained monogamy is how committed the couple is to one another. The greater the commitment, the stronger the potential for sustained monogamy.

Dr. Paula

The study findings don't shock me, but what I do find surprising is that there are so many relationships where the subject of monogamy isn't explicitly discussed. Couples don't seem to enter into any kind of verbal agreement to be monogamous — with the only exception being if they're talking about not wanting to be exposed to sexually transmitted diseases. I find it interesting that one of the main factors that separates a casual relationship from a serious relationship — *exclusivity* — isn't even put on the table for discussion.

Dr. Reef

The majority of the time, if a guy is dating someone but he's not ready to get married, he's not going to call up his girlfriend and say, *"Hey, I was just thinking about monogamy. Why don't we meet up after yoga class, get a mani-pedi, check out the Lady Gaga concert, and talk about where this relationship is going."* If a guy isn't sure about exclusivity or if he's not comfortable having the monogamy talk, he certainly is not going to bring that topic up. *And* he's going to do everything in his power *not* to have that conversation. He'll distract you, change the subject, leave for a few weeks by telling you he has to go on a field trip to Lima, Peru, anything to avoid that conversation.

Dr. Paula

Dear reader, are faithfulness and monogamy important to you? If so, then be honest with yourself. Sometimes women will convince themselves that it is okay for him to see other people. If you spend time seething when checking his Facebook page to see who's commented on his recent pictures, while he's out meeting other women, then you're probably not inclined to liking an open relationship. Just because he wants a nonmonogamous relationship doesn't mean you have to.

A client of mine was in an open dating relationship for several years. Recently, she realized that it's no longer working for her. She used to like having the option of multiple dating partners and genuinely didn't mind if her boyfriend did the same. But things had changed. She was struggling. *"Do I have the right to change the rules now?"* she asked. Of course she does. The key is acknowledging what she wants now. Just because something worked in the relationship before doesn't mean it will work forever. Like the Constitution of the United States, relationships are best when they are living documents open to reinterpretation and change.

Dr. Reef

Paula, did you just really reference the Constitution of the United States in a dating book?

Women, if you ask your boyfriend to be monogamous, be prepared for the answer.

At some point in time, men want to be in a committed relationship. They get tired of dating and may want kids and companionship. The important thing to consider is that men need to come to their own conclusion that commitment is a good thing for them and that it will ultimately enhance their life.

It's all a matter of timing. If you meet a guy who's not ready, you can bang your head against the wall waiting for him to be monogamous — it's not going to happen. You can try to coerce. You can try to manipulate. You can try to bribe him to be faithful. You can take him to couples therapy as long as you want, but he'll only be ready when he's ready.

And the term "ready" for men is not a universal concept. For some men, it's financial security. For others it's fulfilling wild fantasies. For some it's working out past relationships with friends or their parents. Each guy has his own thing to work on prior to being "ready," and he may not even know it.

Sometimes the right woman comes along and the guy instantly "becomes ready," but more often than not, the guy has to be emotionally "ready" to receive that person.

Dr. Paula

Right. The poet Maya Angelou once said, *"When somebody shows you who they are, believe them."* Sometimes a guy will say, *"I'm not ready to get married. I totally want to have a casual relationship. I'm not ready to connect. I'm not good at commitment."* Believe him! You need to listen when they tell you those things. You might think, *Oh, he's a great guy for opening up to me. But things will change.* Maybe things will change, but any changes will be on his terms, not yours.

Dr. Reef

And just because he doesn't want to be in a committed relationship doesn't make him a bad guy. A lot of women have come into my office saying, *"He's not ready to commit. He's such a jerk."* Well, he may not be ready to commit, but you can't take that personally. It's more about the timing in his life than it is about you.

Dr. Paula

Yes, and if that's the case, it means it's not a good fit. It's not about finding a "good" guy, it's about finding the right fit for who you are and what you need. Women do wonder what's going on when a guy breaks up with them, saying, *"I don't want to get married. I'm really not into having a commitment,"* and then two months later he's engaged to someone else. Women ask themselves, *What was that about? Did I prime the pump?* The guy just wasn't interested in you, so it could be taken personally. The key is making a decision about whether you're really good for each other. It's not about who you *want* to be for him or who you *wish* he could be. That's why it's important for women, young and old, to be comfortable with who they are and what they want in order to make a decision about being in a relationship. Otherwise, it's based on dishonesty. Is that what you want the foundation of your relationship to be built on?

A Tip from Dr. Paula

Most women, whether they are aware of it or not, have a mental checklist of what they want and what they don't want. It doesn't mean that the "list" has to be applied to every single guy; each one will have pros and cons. For example, if dating somebody with money is really important to you, but this particular guy has many of the other qualities that also matter to you (sense of humor, hard working, responsible, thoughtful), the money may no longer seem as important.

Name Your Deal Breakers

Terri and Josh had been dating for over a year. When they first started dating, Terri noticed that Josh drank more than she did — in fact, he drank more than most of their friends. But he could hold his liquor and he never became rude or obnoxious, not even when he was on his fifth Stoli. But now that they're starting to talk about living together, Terri is finding it harder to overlook Josh's drinking, especially when he's driving her back to his place. Oh my God, she thought, he could be the father of my kids! He's going to be driving my children around while he's drunk! She shared her concern with him, and he insisted he didn't think he had a drinking problem. She decided to break off their relationship, realizing that heavy drinking was a huge deal breaker for her.

Dr. Paula

Once in a while, the things that might be okay in the early stages of a relationship may not be so in the future. Deal breakers don't always rear their ugly heads at the beginning of a relationship — sometimes we don't become aware of certain behaviors until much later. Also, at the beginning, people may be so enrapt with the new relationship that they may overlook or choose to minimize certain traits in the other person. That's what happened with Terri. There was so much about her chemistry with Josh that was good, she decided the drinking was not such a big deal. But as their relationship deepened and started to get more serious, she become more sensitive to — and put off by — Josh's behavior, which had been there from the start. *He hadn't changed,* but Terri had. Even though they weren't engaged yet, she knew that his drinking was going to be a stumbling block, especially when she thought of him being a father and not driving responsibly. She didn't want him endangering their kids.

Dr. Reef

When we are intoxicated with beauty, charm, and humor after first meeting someone, we overlook many other good or bad attributes. It takes time and less neurochemical hijacking of our brains to see that our love interest is being followed by the cops, has a bookie named Vinnie as his best friend, or is addicted to a stripper named Celeste.

Bad behaviors (drinking, gambling, partying, anger, etc.) are sometimes age related or situational, but they can also be chronic, lifelong problems that you are absolutely going to have to deal with if you commit to this person.

Some people want to rescue others (usually not the healthiest thing to do). Ultimately, Terri realized that Josh's drinking was a definitive deal breaker for her.

It's up to you to figure out what your deal breakers are. The most important part is to think about it beforehand. Ask yourself what behaviors cause you to absolutely not want to date someone. Sometimes, attributes that initially draw you in to someone (impulsivity, always being the center of attention, etc.) become deal breakers later on in the relationship.

Deal Breakers

Everyone has different negative behaviors they can deal with and things they just can't. Are any of these deal breakers for you? If so, why? If not, why not? Be honest with yourself.

- Dishonesty
- Unfaithfulness
- Excessive alcohol or drug use
- Smoking
- Rudeness
- Meanness
- Racist or antigay behavior
- Criminal record
- Excessive debt
- Unhealthy lifestyle

Dr. Reef

Many couples never talk about their deal breakers. The reason could be predicated on fear of rejection. Each fears telling the other the truth. For women, I think their main fear is admitting, *"I want a committed relationship."* They don't want to risk losing the guy, so they remain silent. Women have repressed their desires for so long that it has become a "female" trait.

A typical fear for a guy is getting into a long-term relationship and losing *himself.* As we discussed in Chapter 1, many people have a fear of abandonment or a fear of envelopment. A lot of guys worry they'll get swallowed up if they commit to a relationship. They feel they won't be able to have an individualized identity and they won't have any space.

When you understand yourself better (unfortunately, some people never do), you have a better chance of getting over this fear.

Dr. Paula

I've noticed that the older the woman, the more ambivalent she might feel about moving things to the next level. The more time you spend developing your own life and living it the way you want, the more there is to lose.

Blame It on the Clock

Dr. Reef

When men are younger, they are driven to date, run free, and resist settling down. They don't even want to have the discussion about getting serious, because they're afraid they'll be transported, like on *Star Trek*, to some marriage planet — and all of a sudden they'll have to live there the rest of their lives.

As might be expected, as they get older, things like companionship, raising a family, and being with one person become more and more important. There are always some guys who mature faster in their emotional development and get in a long-term relationship earlier. We also see guys who get in an unhealthy relationship because they weren't ready. Other guys are late bloomers and take a while to develop.

Either way, it's about what ultimately makes you happy. Some guys are really happy being single, while others feel more stable and secure in a relationship. Not wanting a relationship doesn't make you a bad guy. But, as we get older, it's definitely healthier and happier being in a committed relationship.

Dr. Paula

It's hard for women to really admit it, because it feels a bit retro, but part of the push to get more serious comes from the ticking of their biological clock. Of course they could try and override that, but they can't deny the reality of biology (except as it relates to adoption, donor insemination, surrogates, etc.).

Dr. Reef

I totally agree with you, Paula — women do feel the pressure of their biological clock — but how much of a woman's rush to get married is also based on her own fantasies?

Dr. Paula

Well, Reef, as we've discussed earlier, it starts with fairy tales, like the Cinderella story; getting a man to be the Prince Charming. Those fairy tales are powerful stuff to a six-year-old.

I had this conversation recently with a client. She came to my office and was so irritable with the guy she lives with, because he's not living up to this big Cinderella dream she has of having a fulfilling relationship. At one point she said to me, *"You know what? I just realized I'm pissed off at him because he doesn't have the kind of money we need to start and support a family. I have the ability to really focus on my business, which would mean greater flexibility in my schedule and yet not having the health-care and retirement benefits of a corporate job like his, but he's not able to give me the degree of stability I need to have kids at this point in time — and I can't wait much longer for him to get there."* That's what committing is about for many women. Yes, there are some women who have a baby at 47 years old, but that's the exception, not the rule. Women know that it doesn't matter how healthy you are, there's only a finite period of time in which you're going to be able to have kids.

Dr. Reef

Knowing the difference between fantasy and reality can be really helpful. How much of your thoughts about marriage and weddings are influenced by fairy tales, pop culture, or some other fantasy? Are women so focused on the wedding and the "ideal guy" fantasy that they want the wedding more than the actual guy, and this guy just becomes an "actor" in her "wedding movie"? (Okay, your line is "I do" . . . now turn to the camera and smile.) In other words, it becomes more about the process than the person she's marrying. As you can guess, those marriages usually don't last.

Dr. Reef: *Are You Commitment-Phobic?*

---

1) Do you go on a lot of dates but don't commit to anyone?

2) Do you run when you start getting emotionally connected to one of your dates?

3) Have you had a hard time connecting emotionally in your childhood or with past relationships?

4) Are you scared of losing your individual self if you end up in a committed relationship?

Dr. Paula

People run from making a commitment for many reasons, but a lot of it has to do with personality. There are people who are highly commitment-phobic, and it may take them more time to feel okay about being in a committed relationship. Sometimes, it's because they want to be at a certain level in their career, or they want to be financially secure, or they want to travel or write a novel; they may date for many years before they feel they're ready.

Dr. Reef

Some people think being "commitment-phobic" is a personality trait that is expressed in every aspect of a person's life, but that's not necessarily true. There are many men who can commit: they buy homes, cars, suits, gadgets. They go into a store, make a choice, and buy. It's when the emotional component is added to the mix that things get scary — there are so many unknowns connected to making a physical and emotional commitment to another person.

Dr. Paula

Exactly, and then there are some who are serial monogamists. They keep getting into one long-term relationship after another, without ever making a firm commitment. I see it with people who have a high degree of anxiety and risk aversion; this combination can either push them toward impulsive behavior, such as attaching themselves to another person to avoid loneliness, or it can go in the opposite direction, when their aversion to risk flares and it keeps them from making any kind of commitment. Either way, they do not make long-term connections.

Advice from Dr. Paula: *Five Signs of "Commitment-Phobia"*

Here are five key indicators that the person you're dating might be commitment-phobic. Any one of these can have totally legitimate reasons behind it, but if there are too many that apply, you should pay attention. The best predictor of future behavior is past behavior.

1) Frequent change in jobs, colleges, or addresses.
2) History of dating unavailable people (i.e., married, long distance, or secret affairs with coworkers).
3) Multiple exes.
4) Tells you straight out that they are scared of marriage or don't really believe in monogamy.
5) They get anxious or irritated if you want to talk about taking the relationship to a deeper level. But just because they don't feel ready to move in together (or even plan to go to an event in the next month) doesn't mean they are commitment-phobic. Getting mad at you for just bringing up the subject (especially if it hasn't already been discussed) can be a sign of an issue.

Dr. Reef

Many men get married or become exclusive because someone gives them an ultimatum: either commit or lose her. As I mentioned previously, some guys end up committing just because they don't want to lose the woman to someone else. Commitment-phobic men have to figure out a way to know if they really *want* to be in a lasting relationship and are just scared, *or* if they aren't ready for it. If they're not ready, they should keep working on their emotional growth. If they're scared, they need to look at what's stopping them.

MEETING THE FAMILY

Dr. Reef

Meeting your significant other's family can be a smooth, fun experience or a total nightmare. Much of your boyfriend or girlfriend's emotional development has something to do with their parents as well as their influences around politics, religion, money, etc. If the parents like you, it's a relief. If they don't like you or think you're not right for their son or daughter, it creates a stress that some couples can't handle, and it may be the stimulus for a future breakup.

Advice from Dr. Reef: *Things to Do When Meeting the Family*

---

1) Try to fit in. Whatever the discussion or mood is in the room, try to be a part of it.

2) Don't discuss anything of conflict with your significant other — especially in front of the family. If you hate his "dogs playing poker" poster in the basement, don't bring it up here.

3) Be respectful. It's their house and their turf; don't try to change things or be overtly sexual with your boyfriend or girlfriend. Asking if you can have some "private time" in the master bedroom is a bad idea.

4) Compliment your boyfriend or girlfriend. Talk about why you like him or her. Discussing positive attributes about their son or daughter can lead to a bonding experience with them.

5) Offer to help out. Being an active part of the family dynamics (cooking, cleaning up, playing games, etc.) is another potential for bonding.

Your Place — or Mine?

Dr. Paula

There are lots of reasons for couples to consider moving in with one another — from the most wonderfully romantic to the mundanely practical, like my lease is up. Many look at it as a test run — a trial period to see if the arrangement works.

When the decision has been made to live together, you're essentially making a promise to the other person. Monogamy may be a part of the promise, not smoking in the house may be another, separate bank accounts, sharing household duties, splitting expenses, and more — all should be considered before making the move. There's a lot more accountability when you're living with someone as opposed to being on your own. It's natural for the relationship to move to a deeper level.

Dr. Reef

I think living together is good and bad. It can be good if, like Paula said, it's a trial period to test compatibility, and exclusivity, and to have a little more accountability. It's bad because you're not really married.

However you define the contract of marriage, it changes things. When you move in together and are not married, it's like being "pseudo-committed." You're not married, but you're seeing all the dirty clothes on the floor and the dishes in the sink. I've seen many relationships where the couple got married first, before living together, and they were more accepting of each other's difficulties because they had made that commitment. However, for other couples — who decide to live together but not to marry — they often don't have enough of a commitment to help them deal with the other person's challenges, and many ultimately break up.

Dr. Paula

You want to make sure your conversation on this subject covers why both of you want to do this — you want to make sure you're both on the same page. If you're not, are you okay with that? That's when dialogue is really crucial. He might be assuming that because she gave a key or asked him to live with her that she wants to marry him, because that's what living together means to him. Living together is a big step, but it doesn't always lead to marriage.

Dr. Reef

Right, and he might be thinking, *Okay, I really like this woman, and it's a lot easier moving in with her than always driving back and forth from my place. I can see being with her in the future. My only real concern is that I haven't been exclusive up till now — and I don't know if I'm going to be able to be exclusive with her.*

They have two entirely different views of what this arrangement means.

Advice from Dr. Paula: *Are You Planning to Live Together?*

Here are five questions to ask before calling the movers:

1) Is it for reasons *other* than finances?
2) Are you friends?
3) Can you agree on where to live, how much to spend, and what furniture to keep?
4) Do you have good enough communication skills to deal with conflicts when the other isn't pulling their weight in the household chores, is late with their part of the rent, or has an opposite sleep/work schedule?
5) Do you share similar goals? Does moving in together mean the same thing to each of you?

 Gerald and Leigh have been living together for a few months. Since rents in the city are high, the economic arrangement works out for both of them. Leigh figures they're on their way to something more committed, though she hasn't actually brought up the subject with Gerald. For Gerald, such a relationship is the farthest thing from his mind.

Dr. Paula

If Gerald and Leigh have reached the point where they're sharing the bills and Leigh thinks Gerald is the person she wants to be with for the long run, but she hasn't really said that to him, then she's making an assumption that he feels the same way. She could end up being absolutely shocked when she finds out that he doesn't feel the same as her. Leigh has got to look within herself and be clear about what it is she really wants. This is the time for one of those crucial conversations.

Don't be scared to ask for what you want. If it doesn't match up with what your partner wants, you may have to end the relationship. Don't stay with somebody because you're scared of being alone — some of the people who are loneliest are the ones who stay in bad relationships.

······················· **BOTTOM LINE** ·······················

Dr. Paula

Life is filled with big decisions, one of the most important being whom we choose to have a long-term relationship with. While you can never know with complete certainty that you are making the right choice, exploring the truth about who you really are and what you really want will help you make your decision. There are no perfect men or women. But with insight, understanding, and honesty, we get closer to making that "right fit" choice. So often, men and women use the question *"Why do you do that?"* as a vehicle for expressing frustration and anger. *Why* is a powerful word; it can be used as a weapon to inflict pain or as a tool for understanding and greater connection.

My hope is that in the pages of this book you have realized how much power you have over your own relationships and happiness. Curiosity, rather than judgment, is the key. Know yourself. Stay curious. Stop judging yourself and others. You know so much more than you realize. It's important to keep asking *"Why?"* and be willing to listen to the answer.

Dr. Reef

Dating can be fun and spontaneous or anxiety provoking and dramatic. It depends on whom you go out with, the emotional and physical connection, and your previous conditioning and imprinting. What most people don't know is that our emotional past leads to dating habits that often define our future behavior. And most of the time, we have no idea why we react the way we do when meeting certain people. Hopefully, you've "picked up" some valuable information from this book that will enhance your dating life (get it?) — whether those dates lead to a glorious hour or a lifelong relationship. We've enjoyed writing this book, and we sincerely hope you find love and everything else you desire.

Acknowledgments

It takes a village to write a book (and to not go completely insane while doing it). First, I'd like to thank Robin Haywood at Sellers Publishing for conceiving of this project, believing in it, and sharing her editorial wisdom. To Mark Chimsky, who worked with Robin on the editing of this book, for providing the guidance and reassurance this first-time author desperately needed. You showed me, instead of telling me, to trust the writing process and to believe in myself. Thank you, Reef, my coauthor and conversation partner, for being so generous in sharing your experience. Thank you to all the clients over the years who've allowed me the privilege of witnessing your courage. You inspire me. To my Facebook village, for your support, humor, and viral videos. Gratitude to my wise tribe of loving and strong women: Annemarie, Beatriz, Dana, the Denises, Kerri, Laura, Liz, Marybeth, Nicole, Shoshana, Stacy, Stephanie, Terry, Trish, and my mother-in law, Bonnie. Thank you to Tia Mirtha for your love and light. To Ronald, my big brother and lifelong inspiration, for your unconditional everything. To Dad, thank you for teaching me to strive for excellence. And Mom, where would I be without you? Thank you for encouraging me to trust intuition and believe in the big dreams. To Rachel and Isaac, thank you for just being you — being your mom is the honor of a lifetime. And finally to my dear husband, Steve, for your unending support, patience, and love. You are the how to my why.

— *Dr. Paula Bloom*

Being in the position to provide insight on human behavior comes from over a decade of academic training, many years of clinical experience, and a lot of time dating. As such, I'd like to acknowledge all my educators and supervisors in the world of medicine, psychology, and relationship therapy, particularly Dr. Walter Brackelmanns. And I'd like to thank all my good and bad dates over the years. Every date is an opportunity to grow and learn about ourselves, and I've definitely had a lot of growth spurts. Finally, I'd like to thank Robin, Mark, and Ronnie at Sellers Publishing, my coauthor, Paula Bloom, and, of course, my family — my mom, dad, brother, and nephews.

— *Dr. Reef Karim*

About the Authors

Dr. Paula Bloom is a clinical psychologist who's been a frequent guest contributor to HLN's *Nancy Grace Show*, CNN, CNN International, and CNN en Espanol. In addition, she has appeared on Dr. Sanjay Gupta's show on the CNN Accent Health network. Dr. Bloom contributes blogs to *This Emotional Life* for PBS.org and *The Huffington Post*. She has also moderated a PBS-sponsored webinar with Gretchen Rubin, the best-selling author of *The Happiness Project*. She lives in Atlanta.

Dr. Reef Karim is a leader and pioneer in the fields of mental health, addiction medicine, and relationship therapy, and a well-known media personality. He is an assistant clinical professor at the UCLA Semel Institute for Neuroscience and the founder and medical director of The Control Center for Addiction in Beverly Hills. Dr. Karim has appeared on *Oprah, Larry King Live, Anderson Cooper 360, The TODAY Show, Good Morning, America, Dr. Phil, Dateline, Nightline,* and *Chelsea Lately*. He has been featured as an expert in *Cosmo* and *Us Weekly,* and he writes for *The Huffington Post.* As a guest expert, he is interviewed on the DVD of *The Bourne Identity* and he serves as a medical consultant to films and TV. For his work in medicine, advocacy, and entertainment, Dr. Karim was voted one of *PEOPLE* magazine's "sexiest men alive." He lives in Los Angeles.